THE BLUES

2ND EDITION

MELODY LINE, CHORDS AND LYRICS
FOR KEYBOARD • GUITAR • VOCAL

HAL•LEONARD®

ISBN-13: 978-0-7935-5259-7
ISBN-10: 0-7935-5259-1

HAL•LEONARD® CORPORATION
7777 W. BLUEMOUND RD. P.O. BOX 13819 MILWAUKEE, WI 53213

Visit Hal Leonard Online at
www.halleonard.com

Welcome to the PAPERBACK SONGS® SERIES.

Do you play piano, guitar, electronic keyboard, sing or play any instrument for that matter? If so, this handy "pocket tune" book is for you.

The concise, one-line music notation consists of:

MELODY, LYRICS & CHORD SYMBOLS

Whether strumming the chords on guitar, "faking" an arrangement on piano/keyboard or singing the lyrics, these fake book style arrangements can be enjoyed at any experience level – hobbyist to professional.

The musical skills necessary to successfully use this book are minimal. If you play guitar and need some help with chords, a basic chord chart is included at the back of the book.

While playing and singing is the first thing that comes to mind when using this book, it can also serve as a compact, comprehensive reference guide.

However you choose to use this PAPERBACK SONGS® SERIES book, by all means have fun!

CONTENTS

ALL YOUR LOVE
(I Miss Loving)

Words and Music by
OTIS RUSH

AS THE YEARS GO PASSING BY

Words and Music by
DEADRIC MALONE

BABY PLEASE DON'T GO

Words and Music by
JOSEPH LEE WILLIAMS

here, _____

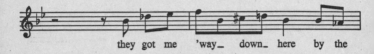

they got me 'way_ down_ here by the

roll - in' fog, _____ treat me like a dog, _____

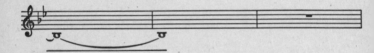

_____

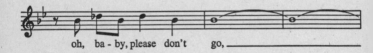

oh, ba - by, please don't go, _____

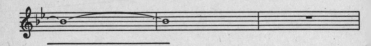

_____

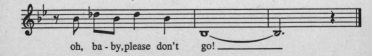

oh, ba - by, please don't go! _____

BEFORE YOU ACCUSE ME
(Take a Look at Yourself)

Words and Music by
ELLAS McDANIELS

Medium Shuffle

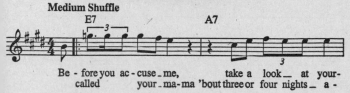

Be - fore you ac - cuse _ me, take a look _ at your -
called your ma - ma 'bout three or four nights _ a -

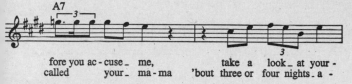

self. _____ Be -
go. _____ I

fore you ac - cuse _ me, take a look _ at your -
called your ma - ma 'bout three or four nights _ a -

self. _____ You said, "I'm
go. _____ Your

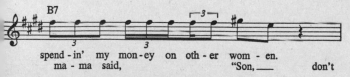

spend - in' my mon - ey on oth - er wom - en.
ma - ma said, "Son, _____ don't

16

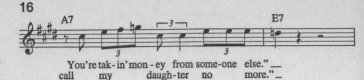

You're tak-in' mon-ey from some-one else." ___
call my daugh-ter no more." ___

1
I
2
Be -

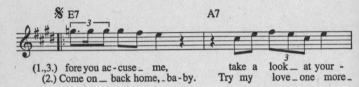

(1.,3.) fore you ac-cuse ___ me, take a look ___ at your -
(2.) Come on ___ back home, ___ ba-by. Try my love ___ one more ___

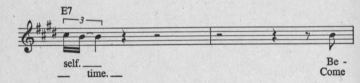

self. ___ Be -
___ time. ___ Come

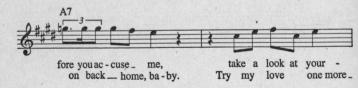

fore you ac-cuse ___ me, take a look at your -
on back ___ home, ba-by. Try my love one more ___

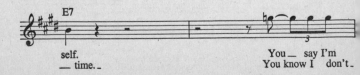

self. You ___ say I'm
___ time. ___ You know I don't ___

BABY WHAT'S WRONG

Words and Music by
JIMMY REED

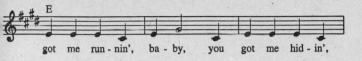

got me run-nin', ba-by, you got me hid-in',

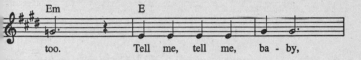

too. Tell me, tell me, ba-by,

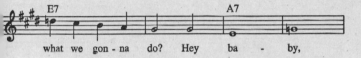

what we gon-na do? Hey ba - by,

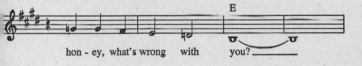

hon - ey, what's wrong with you? _____

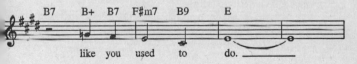

You don't treat me, dar - lin',

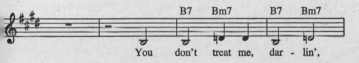

like you used to do. _____

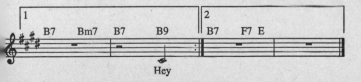

Hey

BACK DOOR MAN

Written by WILLIE DIXON

Moderately
Chorus
E7

I ___ am ___

a back door man. ___

I ___ am ___

a back door man. ___

Well, the men don't ___ know but the

lit-tle girls ___ un-der-stand. ___

Verse

1. When ev-'ry-bod-y's tryin' to sleep, ___
2.-4. *(See additional lyrics)*

I'm some - where_ mak-in' my   mid-night creep._

Just the morn - in'___   the roost - er crow,_____

some-thin' tell _ me _   I got to go._

Additional Lyrics

2. They take me to the doctor, shot full of holes,
   Nurse cried, can't save his soul.
   Accused him for murder, first degree,
   Judge wife cried, let the man go free.
   Chorus

3. When everybody's tryin' to sleep,
   I'm somewhere makin' my midnight creep,
   Every morning the rooster crow,
   Something tell me I got to go.
   Chorus

4. Cop's wife cried, "Don't kick him down,
   Rather be dead, six feet in the ground."
   When you come home you can eat pork and beans,
   I eat more chicken any man seen.

BIG BOSS MAN

Words and Music by AL SMITH
and LUTHER DIXON

BLUES BEFORE SUNRISE

Words and Music by
LEROY CARR

BLUES FOR MY BABY

Written by PETER CHATMAN
(p/k/a MEMPHIS SLIM)

I've got the blues for my ba-by, ev- er since she's been gone.

Got the blues for my ba-by, ev- er since she's been gone.

Rolled and I tum - bled and I cried all night long.

There's on-ly one thing I done wrong, oh, on-ly one thing I done

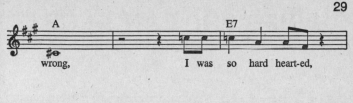

wrong, I was so hard heart-ed,

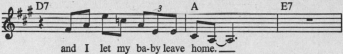

and I let my ba-by leave home. ___

Try-in' to get a - long, ___ the ___ best I can. ___

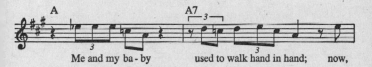

Me and my ba - by used to walk hand in hand; now,

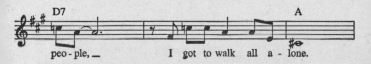

peo - ple, ___ I got to walk all a - lone.

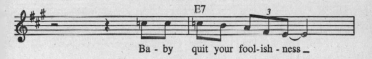

Ba - by quit your fool-ish - ness ___

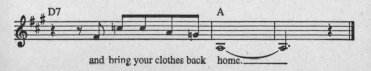

and bring your clothes back home. ___

BLUES YOU CAN'T LOSE

Written by WILLIE DIXON

(Instrumental)

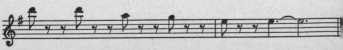

BORN UNDER A BAD SIGN

Words and Music by BOOKER T. JONES
and WILLIAM BELL

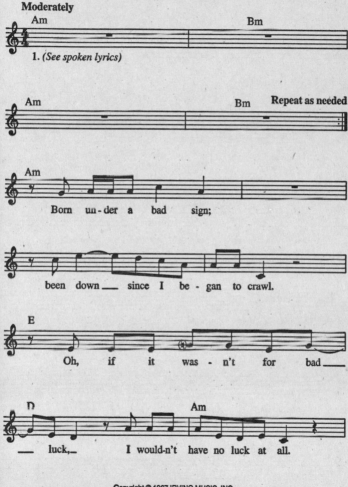

Moderately

1. *(See spoken lyrics)*

Repeat as needed

Born un-der a bad sign;

been down ___ since I be-gan to crawl.

Oh, if it was-n't for bad ___

___ luck, ___ I would-n't have no luck at all.

Bm

(Let _____ me tell you.)

Am   **Bm**

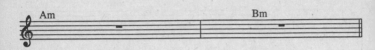

%**Am**

Hard luck and trou - ble   is   my on - ly friend;
I   can't   read; I nev-er learned how   to write.
Wine and wom-en is all I____ crave;

Been on my own   ev - er since I   was ten.
My whole   life   has been one   big   fight.
A big head wom-an will__ car-ry me to my grave.

Born un - der a   bad   sign;

been down __ since I be - gan to crawl.

E

Oh,   if   it   was - n't   for   bad __

(Spoken ad lib.)
I'm gonna get myself together now, I'm gonna keep on pushing.

Spoken Lyrics

1. When I was just a little boy, my daddy left home.
   He left me and my mama to go it all alone.
   You know, the times were hard, but somehow we survived.
   Lord knows, it's a mystery to me how she managed to keep us alive.

2. I've often heard the old folks say,
   "Don't give up, when the chips are down, you got to keep on pushing."
   So I guess I gotta keep on pushing.
   You see, I was down, but I kind of picked myself up a little bit,
   Oh, and I had to dust myself off, clean myself up,
   And now, I'm gonna keep on pushing; I can't stop.

BOOGIE CHILLEN NO. 2

Words and Music by JOHN LEE HOOKER
and BERNARD BESMAN

BOOM BOOM

Words and Music by
JOHN LEE HOOKER

C6
(Shake it, ba - by)
shake, shake it up,
(Shake it, ba - by)
ba - by, come on, now,
F7
(Shake it, ba - by)
ba - by, I don't mean
C
(Shake it, ba - by)
may - be, you're driv - in' me
come on, come
G7
F7
(Shake it, ba - by)
cra - zy, come on, come on.
on, all right, all right..
1 C
(Shake it, ba - by)
Come on and
2 C
(Shake it, ba - by)

CALDONIA
(What Makes Your Big Head So Hard?)

Words and Music by
FLEECIE MOORE

Medium Boogie-Woogie tempo

Walk-in' with mah ba-by, she's got great big feet. __ She's long, lean and lan-ky, ain't had noth-in' to eat, but she's my ba-by __ and I love her just the same. __ Cra-zy 'bout that wom-an 'cause Cal-do-nia is __ her name. __ Cal-do-nia! Cal-do-nia! What makes your big head so hard? But I love you, __

love you   just ___ the   same. ___

___   Cra - zy 'bout that wom - an 'cause Cal -

do - nia   is ___ her   name. ___

___   *(Instrumental solo - ad lib.)*

Cal - do-nia!   Cal -

do-nia!   What makes your big head so   hard?

CHERRY RED

Words and Music by PETE JOHNSON
and JOE TURNER

COLD SHOT

Words and Music by MIKE KINDRED
and WESLEY CLARK

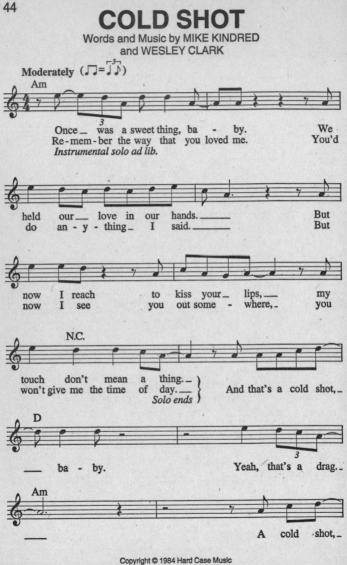

baby.

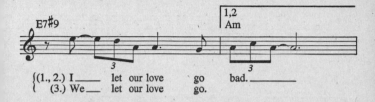

{(1., 2.) I___ let our love go bad.___
(3.) We___ let our love go.

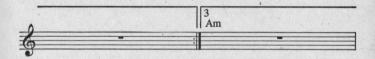

I___ real-ly meant I was

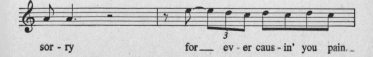

sor-ry for__ ev-er caus-in' you pain.

46

BUILT FOR COMFORT

Written by WILLIE DIXON

Moderately

A7

1. Some folk(s) built like this, _ some folk(s)
2. *(See additional lyrics)*

built like that, _ but the way I'm built (a) don't you

D7

call me fat, _ be-cause I'm built _ for com - fort, _

A7

I _ ain't _ built for speed. _

E7

But I got ev - er - y-thing,

D7

all _____ that a good girl needs. _

Additional Lyrics

2. I ain't got no diamonds, I ain't got no boat,
But I do have love that's gonna fire your soul,
'Cause I'm built for comfort, I ain't built for speed.
But I got everything, all you good women need.

COME ON IN MY KITCHEN

Words and Music by
ROBERT JOHNSON

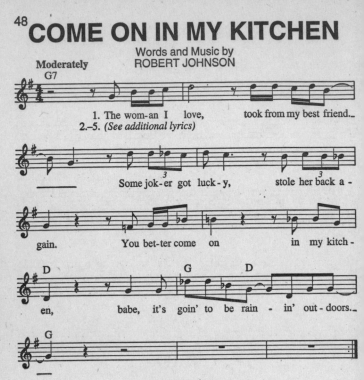

Moderately

1. The wom-an I love, took from my best friend.
2.–5. *(See additional lyrics)*

Some jok-er got luck-y, stole her back a-gain. You bet-ter come on in my kitch-en, babe, it's goin' to be rain-in' out-doors.

Additional Lyrics

2. Oh, she's gone, I know she won't come back.
   I've taken the last nickel out of her nation sack.
   You better come on in my kitchen, baby, it's goin' to be rainin' outdoors.

3. *(Spoken: Oh, can't you hear the wind howl?)*
   Can't you hear that wind howl?
   You better come on in my kitchen, baby, it's goin' to be rainin' outdoors.

4. When a woman gets in trouble, everybody throws her down.
   Lookin' for her good friend, none can't be found.
   You better come on in my kitchen, baby, it's goin' to be rainin' outdoors.

5. Winter time's comin', it's goin' to be slow.
   You can make the winter, babe, that's dry long so.
   You better come on in my kitchen, 'cause it's goin' to be rainin' outdoors.

CROSSCUT SAW

Words and Music by
R.G. FORD

Rhumba feel

1. I'm a cross-cut saw, __ ba-by, drag me 'cross your log.

2., 3. *(See additional lyrics)*

You know I'm a cross-cut saw, __ just drag me a-cross your log. __ I cut your wood so eas-y for you, you can't help but say I saw. __

Additional Lyrics

2. Some call me Woodchoppin' Sam, some call me Woodcuttin' Jim *(2 times)*
   The last girl I cut wood for, wants me back again.

3. I got a double blade axe that really cuts good. *(2 times)*
   I'm a crosscut saw, just bury me in your wood.

COW COW BLUES

Words and Music by
CHARLES DAVENPORT

Moderate Blues

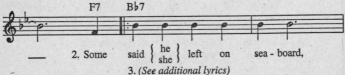

1. I woke up in the morn - in',

my best {man / gal} was gone. I stood at my

bed - side, I hung my head and mourned,

went down the street, I could-n't be sat - is -

fied, I had those rail - road blues,

and I was too dog - gone mean to cry.___

___ 2. Some said {he / she} left on sea - board,

3. *(See additional lyrics)*

some say dou-ble U A, I don't care what train it was it took my { man / gal } a - way.

Eb7
Go starch my jump-er, and i-ron my o - ver -

Bb   F7#5
alls, I'm goin' to ride that train

Cm7   F7   1. Bb
that they call the "Can - non - ball."___

2. Bb
___ She Long."___

Additional Lyrics

3. She blows in Birmingham 'bout half-past four,
   Five o'clock I'm knockin' on my best { gal's / man's } door.
   "Come in sweet { daddy, / mamma, } where have you been so long?"
   "I've been in Cincinnati learnin' how to do the Sally Long."

CROSS ROAD BLUES
(Crossroads)

Words and Music by
ROBERT JOHNSON

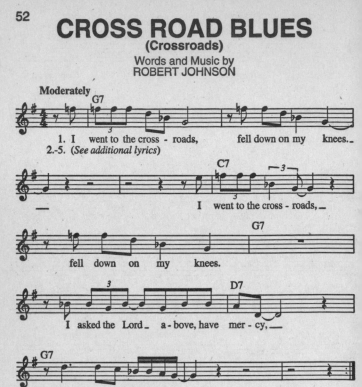

1. I went to the cross - roads, fell down on my knees.
2.-5. *(See additional lyrics)*

I went to the cross - roads,

fell down on my knees.

I asked the Lord a - bove, have mer - cy,

save poor Bob if you please.

Additional Lyrics

2. Standin' at the crossroad, tried to flag a ride. *(Repeat)*
Didn't nobody seem to know me, everybody pass me by.

3. Standin' at the crossroad, risin' sun goin' down. *(Repeat)*
I believe to my souls, po' Bob is sinkin' down.

4. You can run, you can run, tell my friend Willie Brown. *(Repeat)*
That I got the Crossroad Blues this mornin', Lord, I'm sinkin' down.

5. And I went to the crossroad, mama, I looked east and west. *(Repeat)*
Lord, I didn't have no sweet woman, oh well, babe, in my distress.

DRUNKEN HEARTED MAN

Words and Music by
ROBERT JOHNSON

Moderately

1. I'm the drunk-en heart-ed man. ___ My
2.-4. *(See additional lyrics)*

life seems so mis-er-y. ___ I'm the poor

drunk-en heart-ed man. My life seems so mis-er-y. ___

And if I could on-ly change my way of liv-in', it would

mean so much to me. ___ I been dog-___

Additional Lyrics

2. I been dogged and I been driven eve' since I left my mother's home.
   I been dogged and I been driven eve' since I left my mother's home.
   And I can't see the reason why—
   That I can't leave these no good womens alone.

3. My poor father died and left me and my mother done the best that she could.
   My poor father died and left me and my mother done the best that she could.
   Every man love that game you call love—
   But it don't mean no man no good.

4. I'm the poor drunken hearted man and sin was the cause of it all.
   I'm a poor drunken hearted man and sin was the cause of it all.
   But the day you get weak for no good women—
   That's the day that you surely fall.

DARLIN' YOU KNOW
I LOVE YOU

Words and Music by B.B. KING
and JULES BIHARI

Ballad

C — C7

Now, dar-lin'___ you know I love you___ and

F — F#dim7 — C — A7

love you___ by my-self, but you've gone and left

Dm7 — G7 — C — F7 — C — G7

me for some-bod-y else. I

C — C7

think of you ev-'ry morn-in',___ and

F — F#dim7 — C — A7

dream of you ev-'ry night, and I would love

to be with you al - ways. _____ When

night _____ be - gins to fall, I cry a -

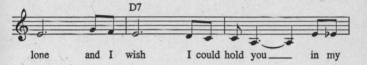

lone and I wish I could hold you _____ in my

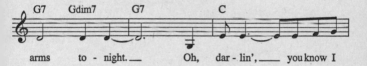

arms to - night. _____ Oh, dar - lin', _____ you know I

love you _____ and love you _____ by my -

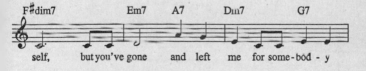

self, but you've gone and left me for some - bod - y

else. _____

DON'T THROW YOUR LOVE ON ME SO STRONG

Words and Music by
ALBERT KING

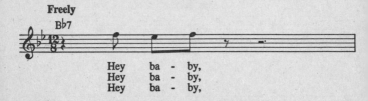

Hey ba - by,
Hey ba - by,
Hey ba - by,

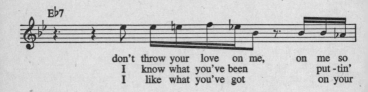

don't throw your love on me, on me so
I know what you've been put - tin'
I like what you've got on your

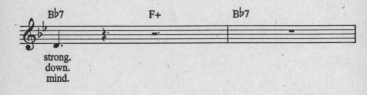

strong.
down.
mind.

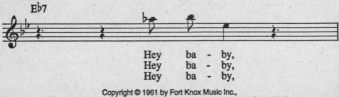

Hey ba - by,
Hey ba - by,
Hey ba - by,

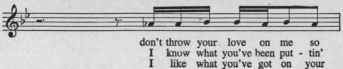

don't throw your love on me so
I know what you've been put - tin'
I like what you've got on your

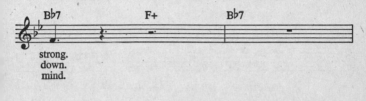

Bb7   F+   Bb7

strong.
down.
mind.

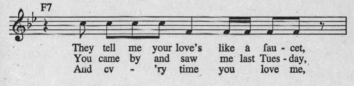

F7

They tell me your love's like a fau - cet,
You came by and saw me last Tues - day,
And cv - 'ry time you love me,

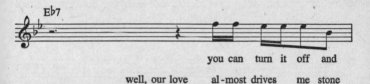

Eb7

         you can turn it off and

     well, our love al-most drives me stone

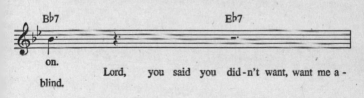

Bb7   Eb7

on.

     Lord, you said you did-n't want, want me a -

blind.

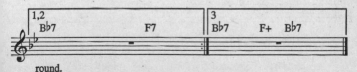

1,2
Bb7   F7   3   Bb7   F+   Bb7

round.

DOUBLE TROUBLE

Words and Music by
OTIS RUSH

Slow Blues

I lay a-wake at night can't sleep just so trou-bled..

It's hard to keep a job, laid off and hav-'n' dou-ble trou-ble..

Hey, hey,

they say you can make it if you try.

Yes, in this gen-er-a-tion of mil-lion-aires, it's

hard for me to keep de-cent clothes to wear.

You laughed at me walk-in', ba-by when I had no place to go.

Bad luck and trou-ble have tak-en me

I have got no mon-ey to show. ___ Hey,

hey, to make it you've got to try,___ ba - by ___ that's no lie.__

Yes, in this

gen - er - a - tion of ___ mil - lion-aires, it's

hard for me to keep de-cent clothes to wear. ___

(Instrumental)

DOWN HEARTED BLUES

Words by ALBERTA HUNTER
Music by LOVIE AUSTIN

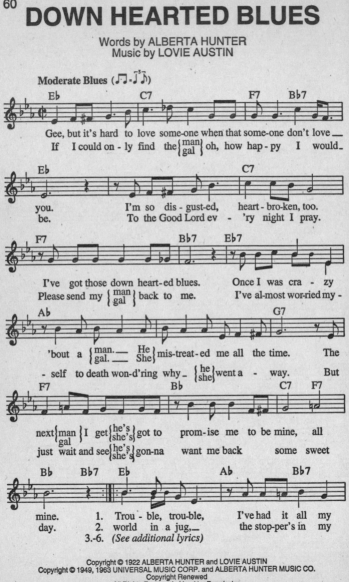

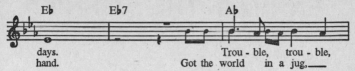

days.
hand.

Trou - ble, trou - ble,
Got the world in a jug,___

I've had it all my days.
the stop-per's in my hand.

It
Going to

seems that trou-ble's going to fol-low me to my grave.___
hold it, ba-by, till you come un-der my com - mand.___

2. Got the
3. Say, I
4.-6.

Additional Lyrics

3. Say, I ain't never loved but three { men / women } in my life.
No, I ain't never loved but three { men / women } in my life.
'Twas my { father, brother / mother, sister } and the { man / woman } who wrecked my life.

4. 'Cause { he / she } mistreated me and { he / she } drove me from { his / her } door.
Yes, { he / she } mistreated me and { he / she } drove me from { his / her } door.
But the Good Book says you'll reap just what you sow.

5. Oh, it may be a week and it may be a month or two.
Yes, it may be a week and it may be a month or two.
But the day you quit me honey, it's coming home to you.

6. Oh, I walked the floor and I wrung my hands and cried.
Yes, I walked the floor and I wrung my hands and cried.
Had the down hearted blues and couldn't be satisfied.

EARLY IN THE MORNIN'

Words and Music by LEO HICKMAN,
LOUIS JORDAN and DALLAS BARTLEY

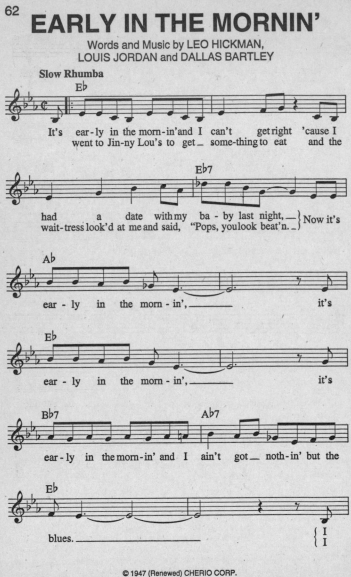

It's ear-ly in the morn-in' and I can't get right 'cause I
went to Jin-ny Lou's to get some-thing to eat and the

had a date with my ba-by last night, —
wait-tress look'd at me and said, "Pops, you look beat'n. —
} Now it's

ear-ly in the morn-in', _____ it's

ear-ly in the morn-in', _____ it's

ear-ly in the morn-in' and I ain't got noth-in' but the

blues. _____
{ I
{ I

EYESIGHT TO THE BLIND

Words and Music by
SONNY BOY WILLIAMSON

And the whole___ state knows she's fine.___

A

Ev-'ry time she starts to lov - in'___

E7

___ she brings eye - sight ___ to the blind.___

A

___ Yes, I de - clare she's pret - ty,

and the whole___ state knows she's fine.___

Man, I de - clare she's pret - ty.___

A9 **D9**

___ God knows. I de-clare she's fine.___ Ev-'ry

A

time she starts to lov - in'___ she brings eye - sight _ to the

E7

blind.___

You're blind.___

1. A   **2. A**

EVERYDAY I HAVE THE BLUES

Words and Music by
PETER CHATMAN

Moderately

1. Ev - ery day,
2.,3. *(See additional lyrics)*

ev - ery day I have the blues.

Oh, ev - ery day,

ev - ery day I have the blues.

When you see me worry - in', babe,

and it's you I hate to lose.

Additional Lyrics

2. Nobody loves me, nobody seems to care. *(Repeat)*
Speakin' of worries and troubles, darlin',
You know I've had my share.

3. Every day, every day, every day, every day,
Every day, every day I have the blues.
When you see me worryin', woman,
Honey, it's you I hate to lose.

FIVE LONG YEARS

Words and Music by
EDDIE BOYD

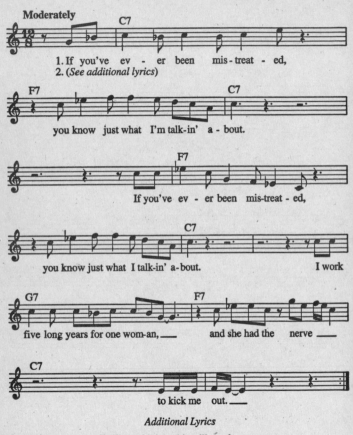

Moderately

1. If you've ev - er been mis-treat - ed,
2. (*See additional lyrics*)

you know just what I'm talk-in' a - bout.

If you've ev - er been mis-treat - ed,

you know just what I talk-in' a - bout.   I work

five long years for one wom-an, ___   and she had the   nerve ___

to kick me   out. ___

Additional Lyrics

2. I got a job at a steel mill, truckin' steel just like a slave.
Five Long Years of fright I'm runnin', straight home with all of my pay.
Mistreated, you know what I'm talkin' about?
I work Five Long Years for one woman, and she had the nerve to throw me out.

FROM FOUR UNTIL LATE

Words and Music by
ROBERT JOHNSON

1. From four ___ un - til late, ___ I was wring -
2.-5. *(See additional lyrics)*

- ing my hands ___ and cryin'. From four ___

___ un - til late, ___ I was wring - ing my hands ___ and cryin'. ___

___ I be - lieve ___ to my soul ___ that your dad-

- dy's Gulf - port bound. ___

Additional Lyrics

From Memphis to Norfolk is a thirty-six hours' ride. *(2 times)*
A man is like a prisoner, and he's never satisfied.

A woman is like a dresser, some man always ramblin' through its drawers. *(2 times)*
It 'cause so many men, wear an apron over-all.

From four until late, she get with a no good bunch and clown. *(2 times)*
Now she won't do nothin', but tear a good man's reputation down.

When I leave this town, I'm gon' bid you fare, farewell. *(2 times)*
And when I return again, you'll have a great long story to tell.

FORTY DAYS
AND FORTY NIGHTS

Words and Music by
BERNARD ROTH

_____ and for-ty nights._____ since_ my

ba - by broke my heart. _____

Search - in' for a lit - tle

while, _ like _ a blind _____ man_ in the dark._

Love can

make a poor man rich or break his heart,_ I don't know

which._ For - ty days_

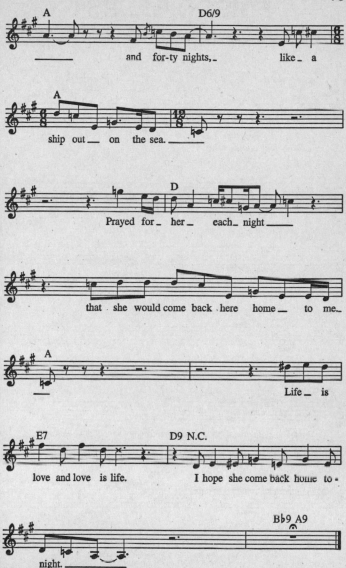

FRISCO BLUES

By JOHN LEE HOOKER

Additional Lyrics

2. That's where
   I wanna be
   San Francisco
   That's where
   My heart
   Up in the New York City
   I've been to Chicago
   But found no place
   Like San Francisco
   With the cable car
   High, high
   On the hill.

3. In the mornin' fog
   The evening breeze
   The cool cool night
   Is where I wanna be
   Oh! Yeah
   Oh! Yeah
   Work, work, you dog
   Tell me about it
   Work out - work out.
   I get the blues
   For San Francisco
   Yes, Yes!

4. My heart is there
   High on the hill
   Right down by
   The Golden Gate
   Across the bay
   That's where I wanna be
   I left my heart right there
   In San Francisco
   With the mornin' fog
   And the cool cool night
   And the cable cars.

FURTHER ON UP THE ROAD

Words and Music by JOE VEASEY
and DON ROBEY

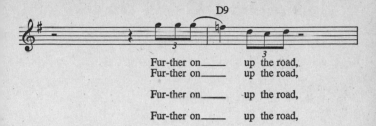

Fur-ther on＿＿ up the road,
Fur-ther on＿＿ up the road,

Fur-ther on＿＿ up the road,

Fur-ther on＿＿ up the road,

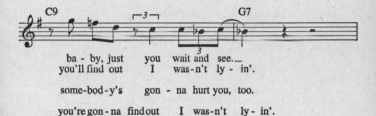

ba - by, just you wait and see.＿
you'll find out I was-n't ly - in'.

some-bod-y's gon - na hurt you, too.

you're gon - na find out I was-n't ly - in'.

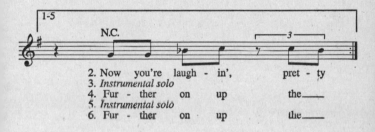

2. Now you're laugh - in', pret - ty
3. *Instrumental solo*
4. Fur - ther on up the＿＿
5. *Instrumental solo*
6. Fur - ther on up the＿＿

GOING DOWN SLOW

Words and Music by
J.B. ODEN

B.B. King narration, spoken over slow $\frac{12}{8}$ blues in B:

Narration:
Thank you so much, ladies 'n gentlemen.
Right here, right here I'd like to tell ya a little story.
This is about a country boy from down home.
This young man had never been north before.

I want ya to listen to me, I got something to tell ya.
He heard about Chicago.
He worked hard all the year, made all of that money,
Eight hundred dollars.

After he gathered his crop, he called his cousin in Chicago
And he said, "Cousin, I'm on my way."
He picked all of that cotton.
I said, this is about a country boy like myself,
B.B. King, you know.

So when he get to Chicago, his cousin meet him and bring him out to the club.
He said, "Set 'em up, cous' is payin' for it."
Had all the go-go girls sittin' out waitin' on him.
They carried him downtown and put him up in one of the plush hotels.

They brought him back out an' said, "Set 'em up, cous' is payin' for it."
His money got a little lighter; they moved him out from the loop
And brought him down to Roberts.
And then he said, "Set 'em up, cous' is payin' for it."

And then the eight hundred dollars, bein' more money than
*   my man had ever had, began to run out.*
Then they moved him out an' put him down to the Persia,
And then, ladies 'n gentlemen, the,
The go-go girls was gettin' fewer,
His friends was fewer.

All his buddies had started to passin' him on the other side of the street.
And then it happened, all his money was gone.
And my man only knew one thing to do.
It was getting cold then, like it is today.
You know what I'm talkin' about.

He went down to the railroad yard,
And one of the few ladies that had helped him to spend his money came by
    to see him.
And she said, "You fool, you fool, I wouldn't have spent your money, but the
    rest of 'em was spendin' your money,
So I decided to spend my portion too, you know."
But ladies, God bless 'em, wonderful somethings, aren't they?

They always like to feel like they're needed.
And she knew my man needed her bad. He'd gotten sick.
He's layin' down there under the boxcar.
Couldn't read so well. So you know, if he couldn't read so well, he couldn't
    write too well.
You know what I'm talkin' about?

So this is the letter, back down home. I know what I'm talkin' about.
It goes like this.

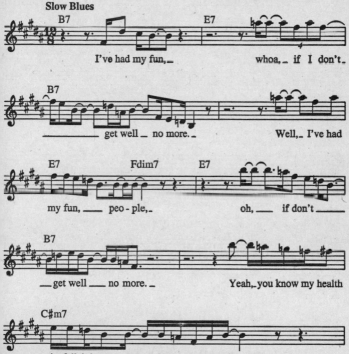

Slow Blues

I've had my fun, __ whoa, __ if I don't __ get well __ no more. __ Well, __ I've had my fun, __ peo-ple, __ oh, __ if don't __ get well __ no more. __ Yeah, __ you know my health is fail-in' on me __ now, __ peo-ple, __

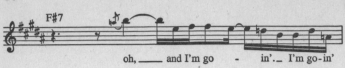

oh, _____ and I'm go - in'. _ I'm go-in'

down _ slow. _____ Yeah, _____

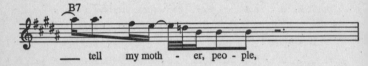

_____ tell my moth - er, peo - ple,

please _ tell her _____ the shape I'm _____ in. _

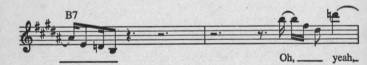

Oh, _____ yeah, _

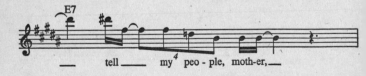

_____ tell _____ my [4] peo - ple, moth-er, _

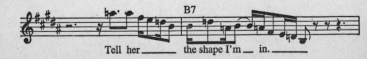

Tell her _____ the shape I'm __ in. _____

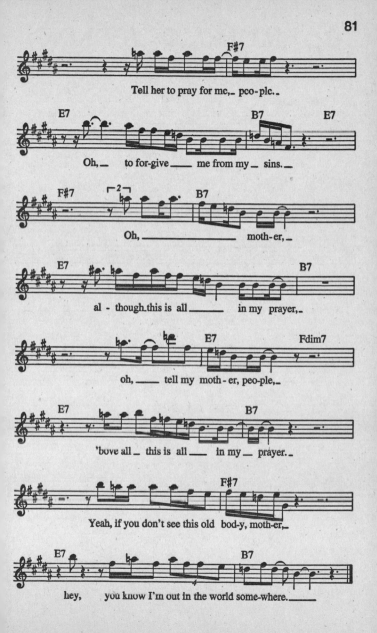

Tell her to pray for me,_ peo-ple._

Oh,_ to for-give _____ me from my _ sins. _

Oh, _____ moth-er, _

al - though_this is all _____ in my prayer,_

oh, _____ tell my moth - er, peo-ple,_

'bove all _ this is all _____ in my _ prayer. _

Yeah, if you don't see this old bod-y, moth-er,_

hey, you know I'm out in the world some-where._____

GOT MY MOJO WORKING

Words and Music by
PRESTON FOSTER

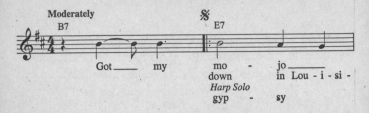

Got____ my mo____ jo____
down in Lou - i - si -
Harp Solo
gyp - sy

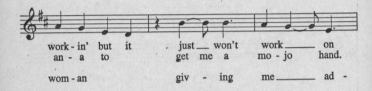

work - in' but it just____ won't work____ on
an - a to get me a mo - jo hand.
wom - an giv - ing me____ ad -

you.

vice.

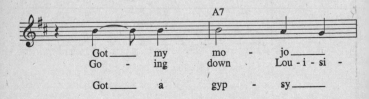

Got____ my mo____ jo____
Go - ing down Lou - i - si -
Got____ a gyp - sy

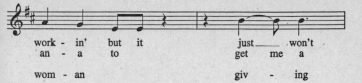

work - in' but it   just___ won't
an - a to   get me a

wom - an   giv - ing

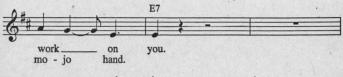

work___ on you.
mo - jo hand.

me___ ad - vice.

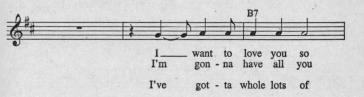

I___ want to love you so
I'm gon - na have all you

I've got - ta whole lots of

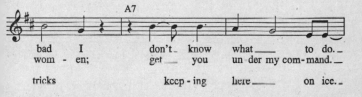

bad I don't_ know what___ to do.
wom - en; get_ you un - der my com - mand._

tricks keep - ing here___ on ice._

GOOD MORNING
LITTLE SCHOOLGIRL

Words and Music by
SONNY BOY WILLIAMSON

Fast Shuffle

A7

1. Good morn - ing lit - tle school - girl,__
2.-4. *(See additional lyrics)*

good morn - ing lit - tle school - girl. __ Can I go

D7   A7

home with, __ can I go home__ with you?

E7

Tell your moth - er and your fa - ther, __

D7   1-3 A7   4 A7

I once was a school-boy, too.   dead.

Additional Lyrics

2. Sometime I don't know what, sometime I don't know what,
Woman, what in this world to, woman, what in this world to do.
I don't want to hurt your feeling, or either get mad at you.

3. I'm gonna buy me an airplane, I'm gonna buy me an airplane,
I'm gonna fly all over shanty town.
If I don't find my baby, I ain't gonna let my airplane down.

4. Now who's that comin' yonder? Now who's that comin' yonder?
She's all dressed up in pretty, she's dressed up in pretty red.
If she don't be my baby, I'd sooner see her dead.

HIDDEN CHARMS

Written by WILLIE DIXON

3. *(See additional lyrics)*

Her lips so sweet, _____ her _____

_____ legs are _____ big, _____ her _____
her love is so true, _____

_____ looks can _____ make you _____
I think a - bout her, _____

that's dance a jig. _____
that's all I do. _____

Her touch is so soft, _____
She's weak as wa - ter,

heart so warm, _____
in my arms, _____

what knocks me out, _____
what moves me, dar - lin',

is your hid - den charms. ___
is your hid - den charms. ___

Her voice is so soft,_ Ooh-wee, what a ba - by!

Ooh-wee, what a ba - by! When __ I hold __

__ her in my arms, ___ brings __

__ out ___ all ___ of her ___

__ hid - den charms. ___

Get it! ___ Her kiss is so pure,_

Additional Lyrics

3. (Her kiss is so) pure, as the morning dew,
   Her gon' love, this Friday, too.
   Oh how they talk, and say come on,
   What kills me baby, is your hidden charms.
   Bridge

HOW LONG, HOW LONG BLUES

Words and Music by
LEROY CARR

HOW MANY MORE YEARS

Words and Music by
CHESTER BURNETT

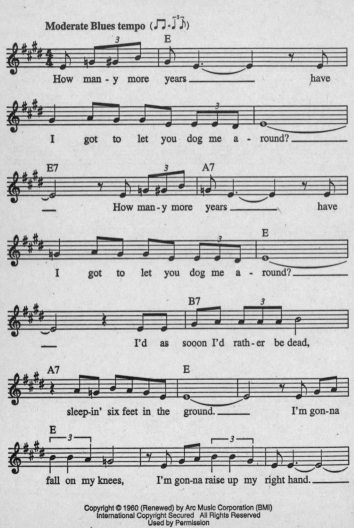

I'm gon-na fall on my knees, I'm gon-na raise up my right hand. _____ Said I'd feel much bet-ter, dar-ling, _____ if you'd just on-ly un-der-stand. I'm go-in' up-stairs, _____ I'm gon-na bring back down my clothes. _____ I'm go-in' up-stairs, _____ I'm gon-na bring back down my clothes. _____ If an-y-bod-y asks a-bout me, _____ just tell 'em I walked out on you.

I AIN'T SUPERSTITIOUS

Written by WILLIE DIXON

Moderate Blues Shuffle

1. Well, I ain't su-per-sti-tious,___
right hand itch-es___
3.–5. *(See additional lyrics)*

but a black cat just crossed my trail.___
I gets mon-ey for sure.___

Well, I ain't su-per-sti-tious, but a
When my right hand itch-es___

black cat just crossed my trail.___
I gets mon-ey for sure;___

Don't___ sweep me with no broom,
but when my left eye jumps,

I might get put in jail. _____
some - bod - y got to go. _____

2. When my

3.,5. Well, I

Additional Lyrics

3. *Repeat 1st verse*

4. Well, the dogs are howlin', all over the neighborhood. *(2 times)*
   That is a true sign of death, baby, that ain't no good.

5. *Repeat 1st verse*

I BELIEVE I'LL
DUST MY BROOM

Words and Music by
ROBERT JOHNSON

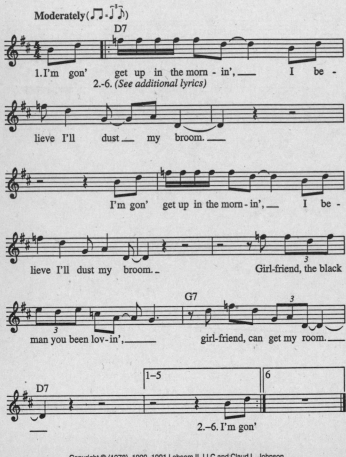

Additional Lyrics

2. I'm gon' write a letter, telephone every town I know. *(2 times)*
   If I can't find her in West Helena, she must be in East Monroe, I know.

3. I don't want no woman, wants every downtown man she meet. *(2 times)*
   She's a no good doney, they shouldn't 'low her on the street.

4. I believe, I believe I'll go back home. *(2 times)*
   You can mistreat me here, babe, but you can't when I go home.

5. And I'm gettin' up in the morning, I believe I'll dust my broom. *(2 times)*
   Girlfriend, the black man that you been lovin', girlfriend, can get my room.

6. I'm gon' call up Chiney, she is my good girl over there. *(2 times)*
   If I can't find her on Philippine's island, she must be in Ethiopia somewhere.

HONEY BEE

Written by McKINLEY MORGANFIELD
(MUDDY WATERS)

Moderately

F7

Sail on, sail on, my lit-tle hon-ey bee, sail on.

Bb7

Sail on, sail _ on, my lit-tle hon-ey bee, sail on.

F7

C7

You gon-na keep on sail-in' til you lose _ your hap-py home.

F7

C7

F7

Sail on, sail on, my lit-tle hon-ey bee, sail on.

Sail on, _____ sail_ on, my lit-tle hon-ey bee, sail on.

I don't mind you sail - in', _____

but please _____ don't sail so long.

All right, lit - tle hon-ey bee.

I hear a lot of buzz - ing. _____

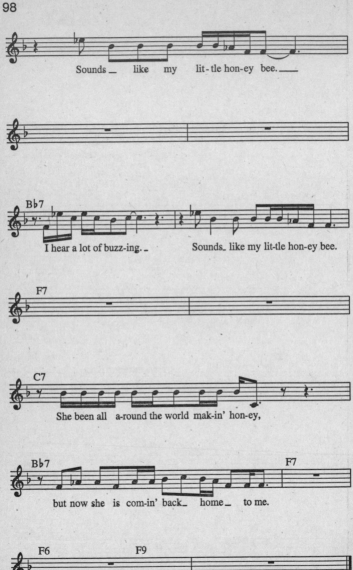

I CAN'T QUIT YOU BABY

Written by WILLIE DIXON

Oh, I, I can't quit you babe, so I'm gon-na put you down for a while. I said, I can't quit you babe, I guess I got to put you down for a while. Said you messed up my hap-py heart, made me mis-treat my on-ly child. Yes, you did, babe.

When you hear me moan-ing and groan-ing, babe,

you know it hurts me deep down_ in-side.

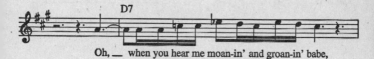

Oh, __ when you hear me moan-in' and groan-in' babe,

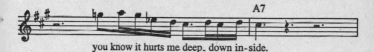

you know it hurts me deep_ down in-side.

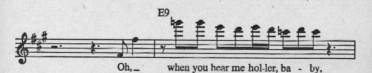

Oh, __ when you hear me hol-ler, ba - by,

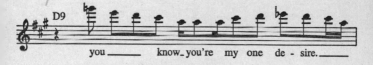

you ___ know_ you're my one de - sire.___

Oh _ yeah, __ Oh!

I'M TORE DOWN

Words and Music by
SONNY THOMPSON

I'm tore down, I'm al- most lev- el with the ground. I'm tore down, I'm al- most lev- el with the ground. Well, I feel like this _ when my ba- by can't _ be found. _

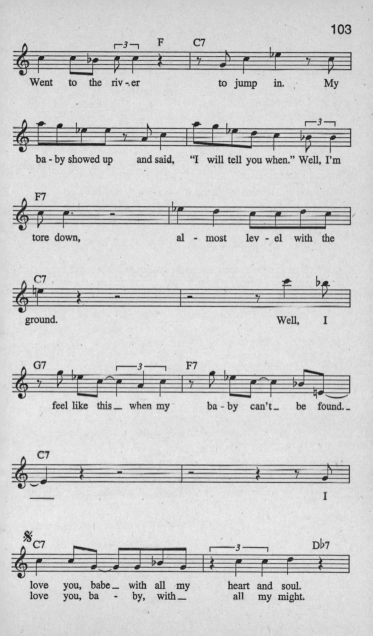

Went to the riv - er to jump in. My

ba - by showed up and said, "I will tell you when." Well, I'm

tore down, al - most lev - el with the

ground. Well, I

feel like this _ when my ba - by can't _ be found. _

I

love you, babe _ with all my heart and soul.
love you, ba - by, with _ all my might.

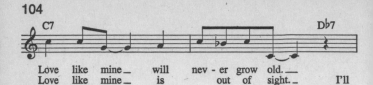

Love   like   mine__   will   nev - er grow old.__
Love   like   mine__   is   out   of   sight.__   I'll

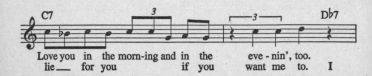

Love you in the morn-ing and in   the   eve - nin', too.
lie__ for you   if   you   want me to.   I

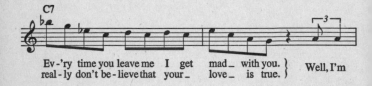

Ev -'ry time you leave me I   get   mad__ with you. }
real - ly don't be-lieve that your__   love   is true. }   Well, I'm

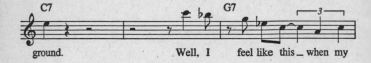

tore down.   I'm   al - most   lev - el   with the

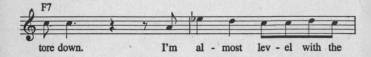

ground.   Well, I   feel like this__ when my

ba - by can't__ be found. __ *(Instrumental)*

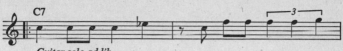

Guitar solo ad lib.

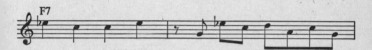

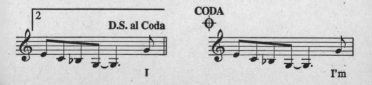

I JUST WANT TO MAKE LOVE TO YOU

Written by WILLIE DIXON

Moderate Blues tempo

1. I don't want you to be no slave, I don't want you (to) work all day, I don't want you to be true. I just want to make love to you.

2. I don't want you to
3. *(See additional lyrics)*

wash my clothes, I don't want you (to) keep our home, I don't want your mon-ey too. I just want to make love to you.

Additional Lyrics

3. I don't want you to cook my bread,
   I don't want you to make my bed,
   I don't want you 'cause I'm sad and blue.
   I just want to make love to you.

I'M A MAN

Words and Music by
ELLAS McDANIEL

Moderately slow

Now when I was a lit-tle boy, at the age of five, I had some-thin' in my pock-et, keep a lot o' folks a-live. Now I'm a man, made _ twen-ty-one. You know, ba - by, we can have a lot o' fun. I'm a man. I spell M. A. _____ N. _____ Man. _____

Ah, _____   Ah, _____

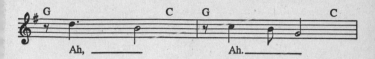

Ah, _____   Ah. _____

All you pret-ty wom-en   stand in line. __

I can make love to you, ba-by, __   in an ho-ur's time.

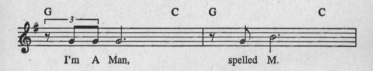

I'm A Man,   spelled M.

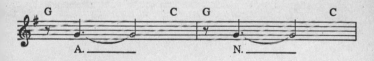

A. _____   N. _____

Man. _____

I'M READY

Written by WILLIE DIXON

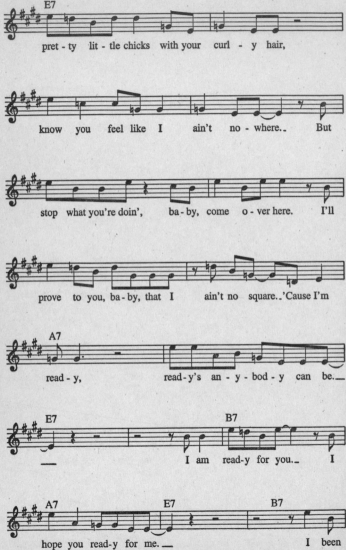

pret - ty lit - tle chicks with your curl - y hair,

know you feel like I ain't no - where.. But

stop what you're doin', ba - by, come o - ver here. I'll

prove to you, ba - by, that I ain't no square.. 'Cause I'm

read - y, read - y's an - y - bod - y can be.

I am read - y for you. I

hope you read - y for me. I been

113

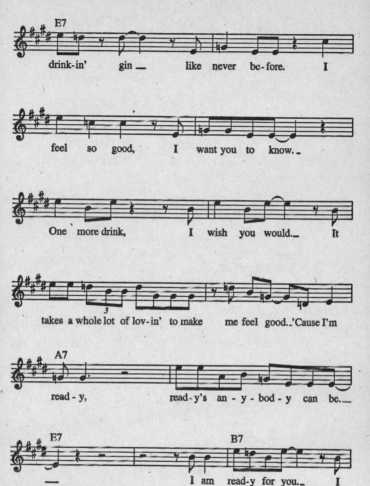

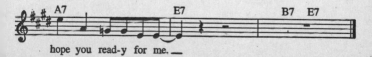

I'M YOUR
HOOCHIE COOCHIE MAN

Written by WILLIE DIXON

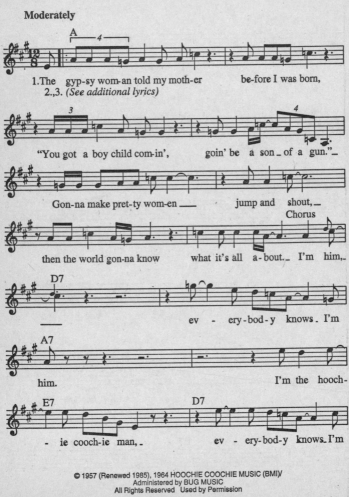

Moderately

1.The gyp-sy wom-an told my moth-er be-fore I was born,
2.,3. *(See additional lyrics)*

"You got a boy child com-in', goin' be a son _ of a gun." _

Gon-na make pret-ty wom-en _ jump and shout, _

then the world gon-na know what it's all a-bout. _ I'm him, _

_ ev - ery-bod-y knows _ I'm

him. I'm the hooch-

- ie cooch-ie man, _ ev - ery-bod-y knows_I'm

him.   2. I

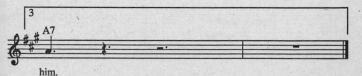

him.

Additional Lyrics

2. I got a black cat bone,
   I got a mojo too,
   I got the Johnny conkeroo,
   I'm gonna mess with you.
   I'm gonna make you girls
   Lead me by the hand,
   Then the world's gonna know,
   I'm that hoochie coochie man.
   Chorus

3. On the seventh hour,
   On the seventh day,
   On the seventh month,
   The seventh doctor said:
   "He was born for good luck,"
   And that, you'll see,
   I got seven hundred dollars,
   Don't you mess with me.
   Chorus

IT HURTS ME TOO

Words and Music by
MEL LONDON

Slow Blues tempo

You say you're hurt, _____ you al-most lost your mind, the man you love, _____ he hurts you all the time, when things go wrong, go wrong with you, it hurts me too.

You love him more, _____ when you should love him less, _____ why sneak up be-hind him, _____ and you take this mess, _____ when things go wrong, go wrong with you, it hurts me

too.

He loves an - oth - er

wom - an ___ and I love you, but you love

him ___ and stick to him like glue, when things go

wrong, go wrong with you, it hurts me too.

He bet - ter leave you, or you got - ta put him

down, be-cause I won't stay ___ to see you pushed a -

round, when things go wrong, go wrong with

you, it hurts me too.

JUKE

**Words and Music by
WALTER JACOBS**

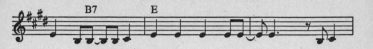

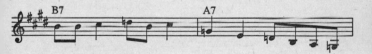

KANSAS CITY

Words and Music by JERRY LEIBER
and MIKE STOLLER

I'm goin' to Kan - sas Cit - y,

Kan - sas Cit - y, here I come

I'm goin' to Kan - sas Cit - y,

Kan - sas Cit - y, here I come.

They got a cra - zy way of lov - in' there and

IF YOU LOVE ME LIKE YOU SAY

Words and Music by
LITTLE JOHNNY TAYLOR

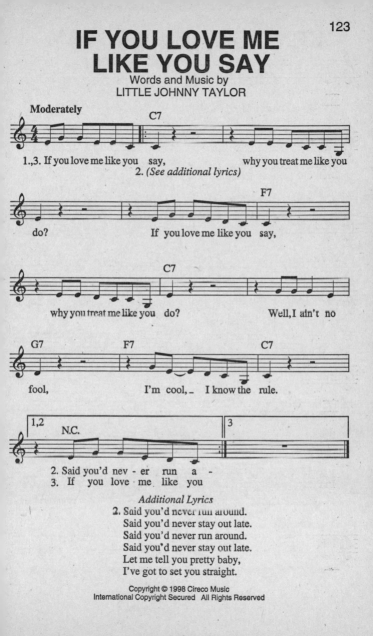

Moderately

C7

1.,3. If you love me like you say, why you treat me like you

2. *(See additional lyrics)*

F7

do? If you love me like you say,

C7

why you treat me like you do? Well, I ain't no

G7   F7   C7

fool, I'm cool, I know the rule.

1,2   N.C.   3

2. Said you'd nev - er run a -
3. If you love me like you

Additional Lyrics

2. Said you'd never run around.
Said you'd never stay out late.
Said you'd never run around.
Said you'd never stay out late.
Let me tell you pretty baby,
I've got to set you straight.

KEY TO THE HIGHWAY

Words and Music by BIG BILL BROONZY
and CHAS. SEGAR

home. _____ Now when the

moon _____ peeks o - ver the moun - tain, _____

yeah, you know I'll be on my way. _____ I'm gon - na

walk, walk this old high-way deep un - til the break of

day. _____ 2. Now gim - me

die. _____

Additional Lyrics

2. (Now gimme) one more kiss, baby,
   Yes, just before I go.
   'Cause when I leave you this time now, baby,
   I declare I won't be back no more.

   So long and goodbye,
   Yes, I had to say goodbye.
   'Cause I'm gonna walk, walk this ol' highway
   Deep until the day I die.
   Chorus

KIDNEY STEW BLUES

Words and Music by
LEONA BLACKMAN and EDDIE VINSON

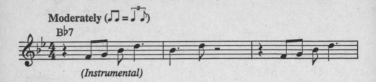

(Instrumental)

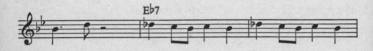

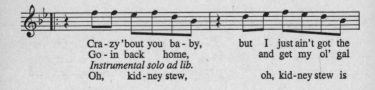

Cra - zy 'bout you ba - by,   but I just ain't got the
Go - in back home,   and get my ol' gal
Instrumental solo ad lib.
Oh, kid - ney stew,   oh, kid - ney stew is

price.
Sue.

fine.

Cra - zy 'bout you, ba - by,
Go - in' back home,

Oh, kid - ney stew,

but I just ain't got the price.
and get my ol' gal Sue.

oh, kid - ney stew is fine.

You're a high price ma - ma,
She ain't the cav - iar kind,

You can save your mon - ey,

To Coda ⊕

so I guess it ain't no dice.
just plain ol' kid - ney stew.

and keep your peace of mind.

1-3

4 **D.C. al Coda**
(take repeat)

CODA
⊕

Bb + Bb6

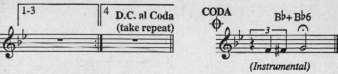

(Instrumental)

KILLING FLOOR

Words and Music by
CHESTER BURNETT

Fast rock

A7(no3rd)

I should-'ve quit you long time a-go.

Instrumental ad lib.

D7(no3rd)

I should-'ve quit you, ba-by, long time a-

A7(no3rd)

go. Yes, I should-'ve, but you got me

E7   D7(no3rd)

mess-in' a-round with you. Ba-by, you got me cry-in' on the kill-ing

A7(no3rd)   E7   A7(no3rd)

floor. If I'd have fol-lowed you

my first night, if I'd have

D7(no3rd)

fol-lowed, pret-ty ba-by, my first

129

THE LEMON SONG

Words and Music by CHESTER BURNETT, JOHN BONHAM,
JIMMY PAGE, ROBERT PLANT and JOHN PAUL JONES

Additional Lyrics

2. I should have listened, baby, to my second mind,
   I should have listened, baby, to my second mind.
   Every time I go away and leave you,
   Darling, you give the blues way down the line.

3. Babe, treat me right baby, my, my, my,
   People tellin' me baby can't be satisfied.
   They try to worry me, baby,
   But they never hurt you in my eyes.

4. Said, people worry I can't keep you satisfied.
   Let me tell you, baby,
   You ain't nothing but a two bit,
   No good, low jibe.

5. Went to sleep last night, worked as hard as I can
   Bring home my money, you spend it, give to another man.
   I should have quit you long time ago,
   I wouldn't be here with all my troubles
   Down on this killing floor.

6. Squeeze my lemon till the juice runs down my leg,
   Squeeze my lemon till the juice runs down my leg.
   The way you squeeze my lemon,
   I swear I'm gonna fall out of bed.

LITTLE RED ROOSTER

Written by WILLIE DIXON

Moderate Blues tempo

1. I am a lit-tle red roost - er, ___ too la - zy ___ to crow for day, ___ I am a lit-tle red roost-er, ___ too la-zy to crow for day. ___ Keep ev-'ry-thing ___ in the barn - yard ___ up - set ___ in ev-'ry way. ___

1,2
3
2. The
3. If

Additional Lyrics

2. The dogs begin to bark and the hounds begin to howl.
   The dogs begin to bark and the hounds begin to howl.
   Oh, watch out strange kin people, the little red rooster is on the prowl.

3. If you see my little red rooster, please drive him home.
   If you see my little red rooster, please drive him home.
   There's been no peace in the barnyard since my little red rooster's been gone.

LOVE IN VAIN BLUES

Words and Music by
ROBERT JOHNSON

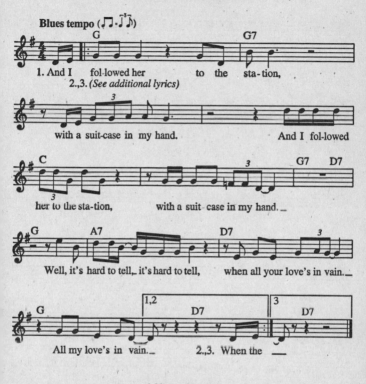

Additional Lyrics

2. When the train rolled up to the station, I looked her in the eye. *(2 times)*
Well, I was lonesome, I felt so lonesome, and I could not help but cry.
All my love's in vain.

3. When the train, it left the station, with two lights on behind. *(2 times)*
Well, the blue light was my blues, and the red light was my mind.
All my love's in vain.

LOVE STRUCK BABY

Written by STEVIE RAY VAUGHAN

Fast Rock 'n' Roll

Well, I'm a love struck ba-by I must con-fess. Life

with-out you, dar-lin', is a sol-id mess. Think-

in' 'bout you, ba-by, give me such a thrill. I got-ta

have you, ba-by, can't get my fill. I

love you, ba-by, and I know just what to do.

I

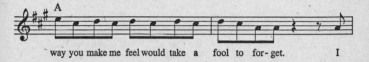

still re-mem-ber, a - let it be said, the

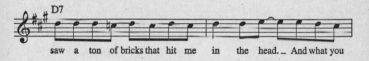

way you make me feel would take a fool to for-get. I

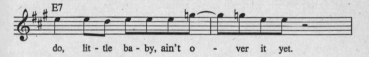

saw a ton of bricks that hit me in the head. _ And what you

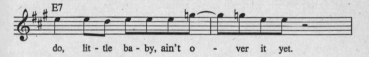

do, lit-tle ba-by, ain't o - ver it yet.

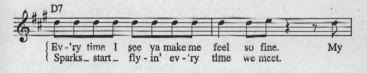

Ev -'ry time I see ya make me feel so fine. My
Sparks _ start _ fly-in' ev -'ry time we meet.

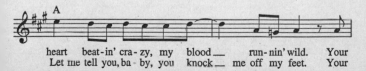

heart beat-in' cra-zy, my blood _ run-nin' wild. Your
Let me tell you, ba - by, you knock _ me off my feet. Your

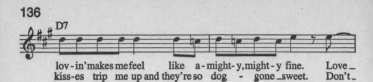

lov-in' makes me feel like a-might-y, might-y fine. Love_
kiss-es trip me up and they're so dog - gone_sweet. Don't_

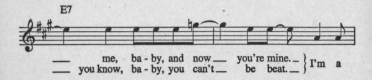

_ me, ba-by, and now_ you're mine._ } I'm a
_ you know, ba-by, you can't_ be beat._ }

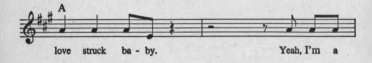

love struck ba-by. Yeah, I'm a

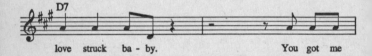

love struck ba-by. You got me

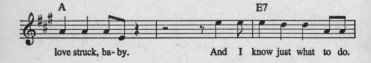

love struck, ba-by. And I know just what to do.

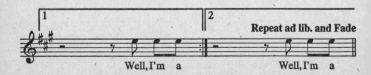

Well, I'm a   Well, I'm a

MADISON BLUES

Words and Music by
ELMORE JAMES

Additional Lyrics

Verse *(Spoken)*

2. I hear your baby's talkin'
   About your Madison shoes
   But I got a song
   Called the Madison Blues.
   Chorus

Verse *(Spoken)*

3. I knew a girl,
   Her name was Linda Lou,
   She told me she loved me,
   But I know it ain't true.
   Chorus

LOVER MAN
(Oh, Where Can You Be?)

By JIMMY DAVIS,
ROGER RAMIREZ and JIMMY SHERMAN

I don't know why, but I'm feel-ing so sad,
The night is cold, and I'm so all a-lone,
Some day we'll meet and you'll dry all my tears,

I long to try some-thing I've nev-er had,
I'd give my soul just to call you my own,
Then whis-per sweet lit-tle things in my ears,

nev-er had no kiss-in' oh, what I've been miss-in',
got a moon a-bove me, but no one to love me,
hug-gin' and a-kiss-in', oh, what we've been miss-in',

lov-er man, oh where can you be?
lov-er man, oh where can you
lov-er man, oh where can you

be? I've heard it said that the

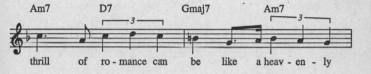

thrill of ro - mance can be like a heav - en - ly

dream, I go to bed with a

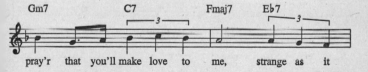

pray'r that you'll make love to me, strange as it

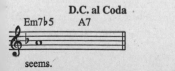

seems.

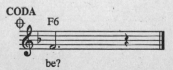

be?

MAMA'S GOT THE BLUES

Words and Music by SARAH MARTIN
and CLARENCE WILLIAMS

141

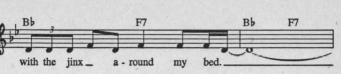

with the jinx — a - round my bed. —

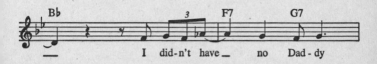

— I did-n't have — no Dad - dy

to hold — my — ach-ing head. —

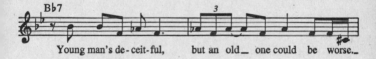

Young man's de - ceit-ful, but an old — one could be worse. —

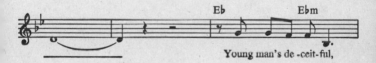

Young man's de -ceit-ful,

but an old — one could be worse. — I'm gon-na get.

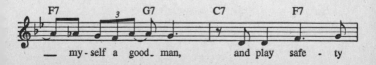

— my - self a good — man, and play safe - ty

MESSIN' WITH THE KID

Words and Music by
MEL LONDON

Moderately fast Funky Blues

1. What this I hear goin' all round town? The
2. *Instrumental*
3., 4. *(See additional lyrics)*

peo-ple are say-in' you're gon-na put the kid down. Oh

no, oh, look at what you

did. You can call it what you want-uh, I

call it mess-in' with the kid.

Additional Lyrics

3. You know the kid's no child and I don't play
I says what I mean and I mean what I say.
Oh, no. Yeah, yeah, yeah. Oh, look at what you did.
You can call it what you want.
I call it messin' with the kid.

4. We're gonna take the kid's car and drive around town
Tell everybody you're not puttin' him down.
Oh, no. Yeah, yeah, yeah. Oh, look at what you did.
You can call it what you want.
I call it messin' with the kid.

MANNISH BOY

**Words and Music by McKINLEY MORGANFIELD (MUDDY WATERS),
M.R. LONDON and ELLAS McDANIEL**

oh yeah,_ oh yeah,_ oh yeah.

man,_____ I'm a man._____ I'm a

full grown man,_ I'm a Roll-ing Stone,_ woo! Oh yeah, oh yeah,_

oh yeah, oh yeah._ *(Instrumental)*

D.S. al Coda

CODA

oh yeah. *(Instrumental)*
Play 3 times

Additional Lyrics

2. The night I shoot will never miss.
   When I make love to you, baby,
   You can't resist.
   I'm a man; spelled M., A., (child).
   N. No B., O., (child), Y.
   That spells mannish boy.
   Chorus

3. All you pretty women,
   Stand in line.
   I'll make love to you, baby,
   In an hour's time.
   I'm a man, I'm a man,
   Oh yeah, oh yeah,
   Oh yeah, oh yeah.

MEAN OLD WORLD

By WALTER JACOBS

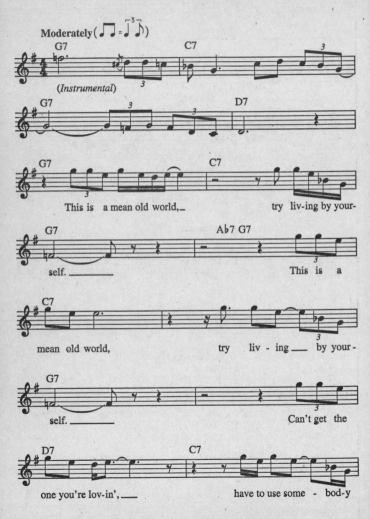

Moderately

(Instrumental)

This is a mean old world,— try liv-ing by your-self.— This is a mean old world, try liv-ing— by your-self.— Can't get the one you're lov-in', — have to use some - bod-y

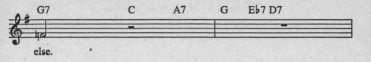

else.

I've got the blues, gon-na pack my bags and

go. _____ Yes,

I've got the blues, _ gon - na pack my bags and

go. _____ Yes, I

guess you real-ly don't love me, I'm just an un-luck-y so and

so. _____

MEAN TO ME

Lyric and Music by FRED E. AHLERT
and ROY TURK

You're mean to me. __ Why must __ you be
mean to me? __ Gee, hon - ey it
seems to me __ you love to see __ me
cry - in'. I don't know why __
I stay home __ each night __ when you
say you'll phone __ you don't __ and I'm
left a - lone __ sing - in' the blues __ and

MELLOW DOWN EASY

Written by WILLIE DIXON

Moderate Blues tempo

1. You jump, jump here, ___

___ you jump, jump there; ___

___ you jump, jump,

jump ev - 'ry -

where. Then you mel - low down

eas - y,

2., 3. (*See additional lyrics*)

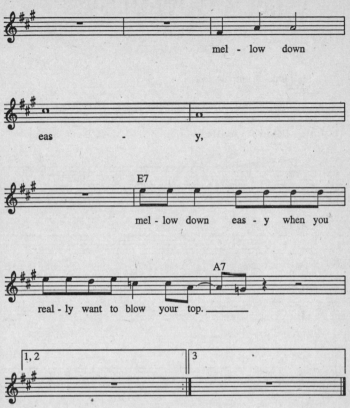

mel - low down

eas - y,

E7

mel - low down eas - y when you

A7

real - ly want to blow your top. _____

1, 2   3

Additional Lyrics

2. Shake, shake here; shake, shake there;
   You shake, shake, shake, everywhere.
   Then you mellow down easy, mellow down easy.
   You mellow down easy when you really want to blow your top.

3. You wiggle, wiggle here; you wiggle, wiggle there;
   You wiggle, wiggle, wiggle, everywhere.
   Then you mellow down easy, mellow down easy.
   You mellow down easy when you really want to blow your top.

MILK COW BLUES

Words and Music by
KOKOMO ARNOLD

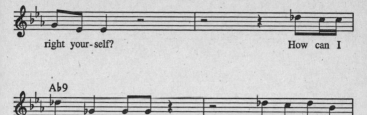

right your-self? How can I

do right, ba - by, when you won't do

right your - self? ___ If

my good gal quits me, ___ Lord, I don't

want no - bod - y else. Well, I

woke up this morn-in', looked out my door,

and I know my milk cow ___ by the way she lows. _ If you

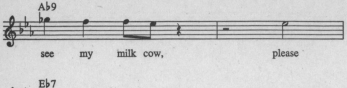

see my milk cow, please

drive her home. ___ I ain't

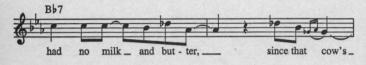

had no milk ___ and but-ter, ___ since that cow's ___

___ been gone. _____

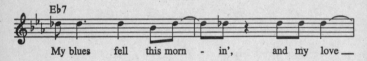

My blues fell this morn - in', and my love ___

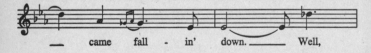

___ came fall - in' down. ___ Well,

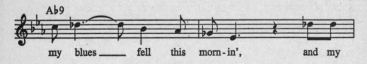

my blues ___ fell this morn-in', and my

love came fall - in' down. ___ I may

be a low-down dog, ma - ma, but please

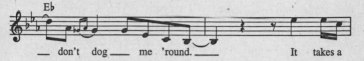

don't dog me 'round. It takes a

rock-in' chair to rock, a rub-ber ball to roll,

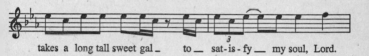

takes a long tall sweet gal to sat-is-fy my soul, Lord.

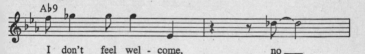

I don't feel wel - come, no

place I go. Well,

the wom-an I love has done drove me from her

door.

MY BABE

Written by WILLIE DIXON

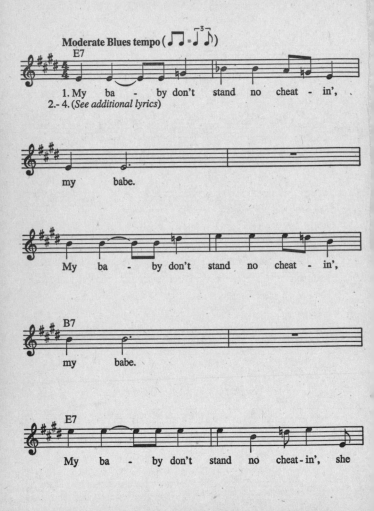

Moderate Blues tempo

1. My ba - by don't stand no cheat - in',
2.- 4. *(See additional lyrics)*

my   babe.

My   ba - by don't   stand   no   cheat - in',

my   babe.

My   ba - by don't   stand   no   cheat - in',   she

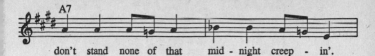

don't stand none of that mid - night creep - in'.

My babe, true lit - tle ba - by, ___

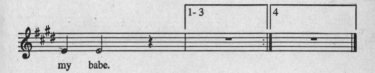

my babe.

Additional Lyrics

2. My babe, I know she love me, my babe. *(2 times)*
   Oh yeah, I know she love me.
   She don't do nothing but kiss and hug me.
   My babe, true little baby, my babe.

3. My babe, she don't stand no cheatin', my babe. *(2 times)*
   Oh no, she don't stand no cheatin'.
   Everything she do she do so pleasin'.
   My babe, true little baby, my babe.

4. My baby don't stand no fooling, my babe. *(2 times)*
   My baby don't stand no foolin'.
   When she's hot there ain't no coolin'.
   My babe, true little baby, my babe.

NOBODY KNOWS YOU WHEN YOU'RE DOWN AND OUT

Words and Music by
JIMMIE COX

Medium Blues tempo

I once lived the life of a mil - lion - aire, __
spend-ing my mon - ey, I did - n't care, __
al - ways tak-ing my friends out for a good time, __
buy - ing cham - pagne, __ gin and wine. __ But
just as soon __ as my dough got low, __ I
could-n't find a friend, no place I'd go. __ If I
ev - er get my hands on a dol - lar a - gain, __ I'm gon-na

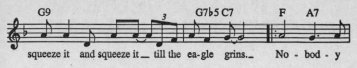

squeeze it and squeeze it __ till the ea-gle grins.__ No - bod - y

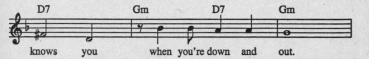

knows you when you're down and out.

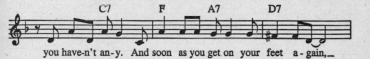

In your pock-et, not one pen-ny, and your friends

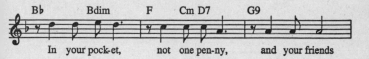

you have-n't an-y. And soon as you get on your feet a-gain,__

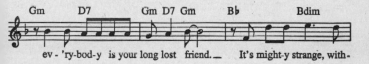

ev - 'ry-bod-y is your long lost friend.__ It's might-y strange, with-

out a doubt,__ but no-bod-y wants you __ when you're down and out.__

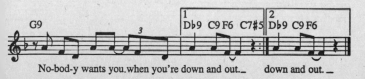

No-bod-y wants you. when you're down and out.__ down and out. __

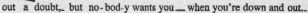

ONE BOURBON,
ONE SCOTCH, ONE BEER

Words and Music by
JOHN LEE HOOKER

One bour-bon,— one scotch and one beer.— One bour-bon,— one scotch and one beer.— Hey, Mis-ter Bar-ten-der— come here I want an-oth-er drink and I want it now, my ba-by's— she gone,— — she can be gone to-night.— I ain't seen my

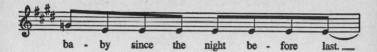

ba - by   since   the   night   be - fore   last. __

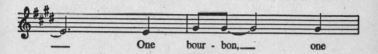

__   One   bour - bon, __   one

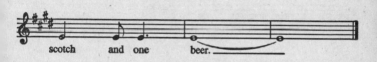

scotch   and one   beer. _____

Additional Lyrics

NARRATION

1. I better not sit there, gettin' high, mellow,
   Knocked out, feelin' good;
   About that time I looked on the wall
   At the old clock on the wall;
   About that time it was ten-thirty then.
   I looked down the bar at the bartender, he said,
   "What do you want down there?"
   Chorus

2. And I sat there gettin' high, stoned, knocked out.
   About that time I looked at the wall
   At the old clock up there.
   About that time it was a quarter to two,
   The last call for alcohol. I said,
   "Hey, Mister Bartender."
   "What do you want?"
   Chorus

PINETOP'S BLUES

Words and Music by
PINETOP SMITH

Medium Blues tempo

Now my wom - an's got a heart like a rock

cast down in the sea,

now my wom - an's got a heart like a rock

cast down in the sea.

She thinks she can love

ev - 'ry - bod - y and

mis - treat poor me.

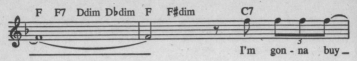

F F7 Ddim Dbdim F F#dim   C7

I'm gon - na buy

F   Bb7

my - self a grave - yard of my own,

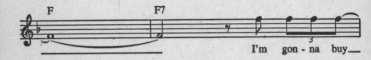

F   F7

I'm gon - na buy

Bb7

my - self a grave -

yard of my own.

F

I'm gon - na bur -

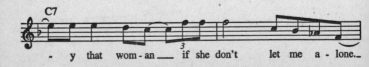

C7

y that wom - an if she don't let me a - lone.

I can't use

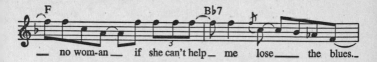

no wom-an if she can't help me lose the blues.

I can't use

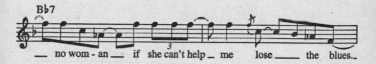

no wom-an if she can't help me lose the blues.

Go-in' down

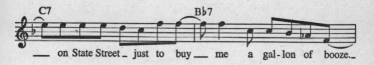

on State Street just to buy me a gal-lon of booze.

PRIDE AND JOY

Written by STEVIE RAY VAUGHAN

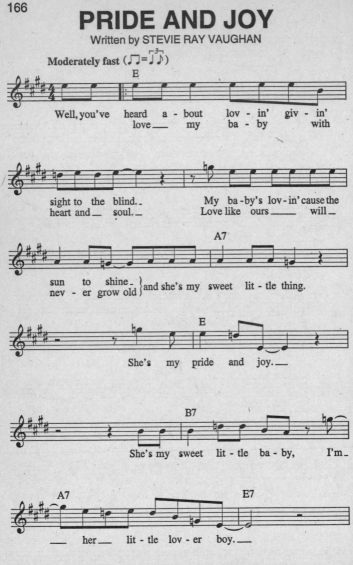

Moderately fast

Well, you've heard a-bout lov-in' giv-in'
love___ my ba-by with

sight to the blind.___ My ba-by's lov-in' 'cause the
heart and___ soul.___ Love like ours___ will___

sun to shine___
nev-er grow old } and she's my sweet lit-tle thing.

She's my pride and joy.___

She's my sweet lit-tle ba-by, I'm___

___ her___ lit-tle lov-er boy.___

Yeah, I

Yeah, I

love my la - dy, she's long and_ lean._
love my ba - by like the fin - est_ wine._

You mess with her, you'll see a man get mean._ } Yes, she's my
Stick with her_ un - til the end of time._

sweet lit - tle thing. She's my

pride and joy._ She's my

sweet lit - tle ba - by, I'm_ her_ lit - tle lov - er boy._

To Coda

_

Guitar solo ad lib.

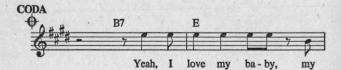

Well, I

CODA

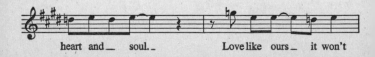

Yeah, I love my ba-by, my

heart and soul. Love like ours it won't

NO PARTICULAR PLACE TO GO

Words and Music by
CHUCK BERRY

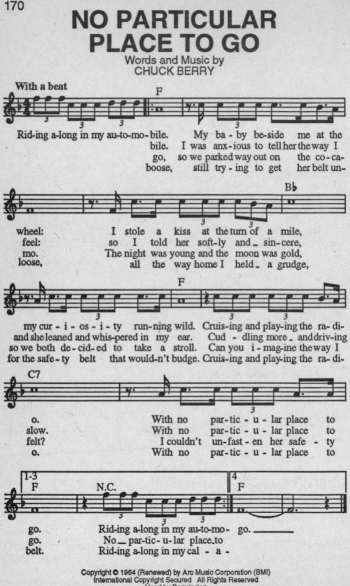

With a beat

Rid-ing a-long in my au-to-mo-bile. My ba-by be-side me at the
bile. I was anx-ious to tell her the way I
go, so we parked way out on the co-ca-
boose, still try-ing to get her belt un-

wheel: I stole a kiss at the turn of a mile,
feel: so I told her soft-ly and _ sin-cere,
mo. The night was young and the moon was gold,
loose, all the way home I held _ a grudge,

my cur-i-os-i-ty run-ning wild. Cruis-ing and play-ing the ra-di-
and she leaned and whis-pered in my ear. Cud-dling more _ and driv-ing
so we both de-cid-ed to take a stroll. Can you i-mag-ine the way I
for the safe-ty belt that would-n't budge. Cruis-ing and play-ing the ra-di-

o. With no par-tic-u-lar place to
slow. With no par-tic-u-lar place to
felt? I couldn't un-fast-en her safe-ty
o. With no par-tic-u-lar place to

go. Rid-ing a-long in my au-to-mo- go. _____
go. No _ par-tic-u-lar place to
belt. Rid-ing a-long in my cal-a-

RAMBLIN' ON MY MIND

Words and Music by
ROBERT JOHNSON

Moderate Blues tempo

1. I got ram-blin',___ I got ram-blin' on my mind.___
2.-4. *(See additional lyrics)*

I got ram-blin',___ I got ram-blin' on my mind. Hate to leave my ba-by, but she treats me so un-kind.___

2. I got

Additional Lyrics

2. I got mean things, I got mean things all on my mind. *(2 times)*
   Hate to leave you here, babe, but you treat me so unkind.

3. Runnin' down to the station, catch the first mail train I see. *(2 times)*
   I got the blues about Miss so-and-so, and the child's got the blues about me.

4. I'm leaving this morning with my arms fold up and cryin'. *(2 times)*
   I hate to leave my baby, but she treats me so unkind.

RECONSIDER BABY

Words and Music by
LOWELL FULSON

With a beat

So long, _____ oh, how I hate to see you go. _____ So long, _____ oh, how I hate to see you go. _____ And the way that I will miss you, I guess you will nev-er know. _____ { We've been to - { You said you

Bb7

geth - er so long, ___ to have to sep - a - rate ___ this
once _ did love _ me, but now I guess you have changed your

F

way. _____ We've been to -
mind. _____ You said you

Bb9

geth - er too long, ___ to have to sep - a - rate ___ this
once _ did love _ me, but now I guess you have changed your

F   **F#dim7**

way. _____ I'm gon - na let you
mind. _____ Why don't _ you _

Gm7   **1. C7**

go a - head on, ba - by, pray that you'll come back home some
re - con - sid - er, ba - by,

F   **2. C7**

day. __ So give your - self just a lit - tle more

F **F7** **Bb** **Bdim7** **F** **Gb7** **F**

time. _____

ROCK ME BABY

**Words and Music by B.B. KING
and JOE BIHARI**

1. Rock me ba - by, rock me all night long.
2. *(See additional lyrics)*

Rock me ba - by, rock me all night long.

I want you to rock me ba - by, like my back ain't got no bone.

Roll me ba - by, like you roll a wag - on

wheel.

Roll me ba - by, like you roll a wag - on

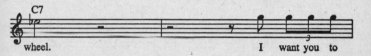

wheel. I want you to

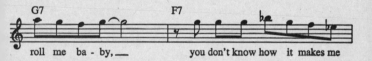

roll me ba - by, ___ you don't know how it makes me

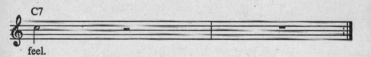

feel.

Additional Lyrics

2. Rock me baby, honey rock me slow.
   Rock me baby, honey rock me slow.
   Rock me baby, till I want no more.

   Roll me baby, like you roll a wagon wheel.
   Roll me baby, like you roll a wagon wheel.
   I want you to roll me baby, you don't know how it makes me feel.

ROLL 'EM PETE

Words and Music by PETE JOHNSON
and JOE TURNER

Medium Blues

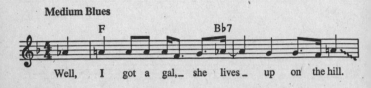

Well, I got a gal,__ she lives__ up on the hill.

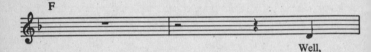

Well,

I got a gal, she lives__ up on the hill.

Well, this

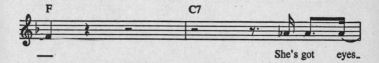

wom-an's tryin' to quit me, Lord, ___ but I love ___ her still. ___

___ She's got eyes ___

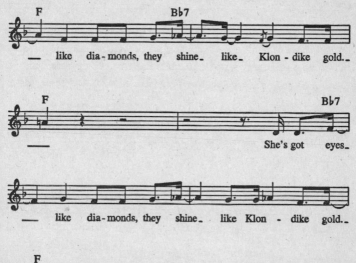

___ like dia-monds, they shine ___ like Klon-dike gold. ___

___ She's got eyes ___

___ like dia-monds, they shine ___ like Klon-dike gold. ___

___ Ev - 'ry

time she loves ___ me, she sends ___ my mel - low soul. ___

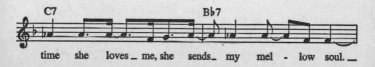

Well, you're so beau - ti - ful, you've got to die some - day. Well, you're so beau - ti - ful, but you've got to die some day. All I want's a lit - tle lov - ing, just be - fore you pass a - way.

Additional Lyrics

Pretty baby, I'm goin' away and leave you by yourself,
Pretty baby, I'm goin' away and leave you by yourself,
You've mistreated me, now you can mistreat somebody else.

ROLLIN' AND TUMBLIN'

Written by McKINLEY MORGANFIELD
(MUDDY WATERS)

(Instrumental)

Well now, come here, ba - by,

sit down on dad - dy's knee.___ (Instrumental)

I wan - na

tell you a - bout __ the ___ way __ they treat - ed me. __

_____ (Instrumental)

(Guitar solo)

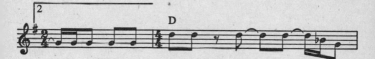

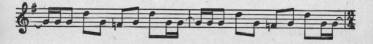

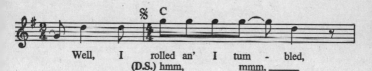

Well, I rolled an' I tum - bled,
(D.S.) hmm, mmm, _____

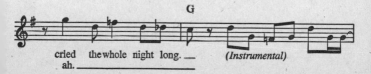

cried the whole night long. ___ (Instrumental)
ah. ___

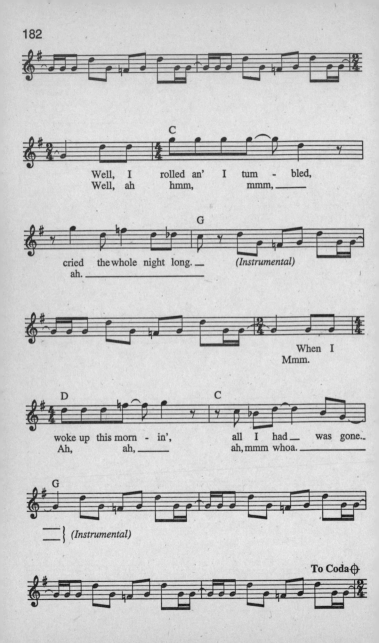

Well, I rolled an' I tum - bled,
Well, ah hmm, mmm, ___

cried the whole night long. ___ *(Instrumental)*
ah. ___

When I
Mmm.

woke up this morn - in', all I had ___ was gone..
Ah, ah, ___ ah, mmm whoa. ___

(Instrumental)

To Coda⊕

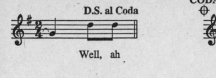

Well, ah

(Guitar solo)

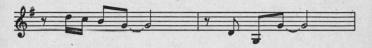

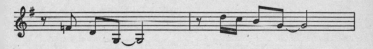

Repeat ad lib.

(Solo ends)

ROUTE 66

By BOBBY TROUP

If you ____ ev - er plan to mo - tor west, ___ trav - el my way, take the high-way that's the best. ___ Get your kicks on Route ___ Six - ty - six! It winds ____ from Chi - ca - go to L. A., ___ more than two ____ thou - sand miles all the way.

185

F6 · Gm7
Get your kicks on

C9 · F · Abdim7
Route ___ Six - ty - six! ___

Gm7 · C7 · F7
Now you go thru Saint Loo - ey and

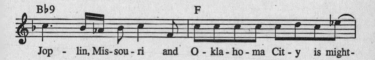
Bb9 · F
Jop - lin, Mis - sou - ri and O - kla - ho - ma Cit - y is might-

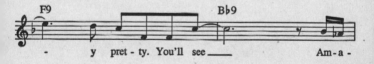
F9 · Bb9
- y pret - ty. You'll see ___ Am - a -

F7 · 3
ril - lo; ___ Gal - up, New

Gm · C9
Mex - i - co; ___ Flag-staff, Ar - i - zo - na;

ROLLIN' STONE
(Catfish Blues)

Written by McKINLEY MORGANFIELD
(MUDDY WATERS)

Moderate Blues beat

E7

1. Well, I wished __ I was a cat-fish, swim-min' in the __
2.-4. *(See additional lyrics)*

__ deep blue sea. __ I would have all __

__ you good look-in' wom-en fish-in', fish-in' af - ter me, __

shaw' nuf af-ter me, __ shaw' nuf af - ter me. __

Oh Lord, Oh Lord, shaw' nuf.

Additional Lyrics

2. I went my baby's house, and I sit down on her sill.
   She said, "Come on in (Muddy), my mother's just not well."
   Shaw' nuf, just not well,
   Shaw' nuf, just not well.
   Oh, Lord, oh, well.

3. Well, my mother told my father just before I was born,
   "I got a boy child comin',
   Gonna be a rolling stone." *(3 times)*
   Oh, well, he's a...

4. Well, I feel, yes I feel, baby, like my lowdown time ain't long.
   I'm gonna cut the twist train, Spokane bound.
   Back down the road I'm goin', boy. *(3 times)*
   Shaw' nuf.

SEE SEE RIDER

Words and Music by
MA RAINEY

SPOONFUL

Written by WILLIE DIXON

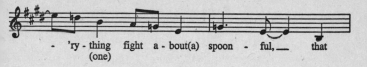

- 'ry - thing fight a - bout(a) spoon - ful, ___ that
(one)

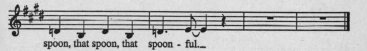

spoon, that spoon, that spoon - ful.___

Additional Lyrics

It could be a spoonful of coffee, it could be a spoonful of tea,
But a little spoon of your precious love is good enough for me.

Men lies about that (spoonful),
Some of them dies about that (spoonful),
Some of them cries about that (spoonful),
But everybody fight about that spoonful,
That spoon, that spoon, that spoonful.

It could be spoonful of water, saved from that desert sand,
But one spoon of luck from my little forty-five, save from another man.

SAINT JAMES INFIRMARY

Words and Music by
JOE PRIMROSE

Slow Blues tempo

I went down to the St. James In-fir-m'ry to
down to old Joe's bar-room, on the

see my ba - by there. She was
cor - ner by the square; they were

ly - in' on a long white ta - ble, so
serv - in' the drinks as u - sual, and the

sweet, so cool, so fair. 2. Went
u - su - al crowd was there. 4. On my

up to see the doc - tor. "She's ver - y low," he
left stood Joe Mc - Ken - ne - dy, his eyes blood-shot

said. Went back to see my ba - by; great
red; he turned to the crowd a - round him, these

God! She was ly - in' there dead. 3. I went
are the words he said: 5. Let her

ST. LOUIS BLUES

from BIRTH OF THE BLUES

Words and Music by
W.C. HANDY

Additional Lyrics

2. Been to the Gypsy to get my fortune told,
   To the Gypsy, to get my fortune told.
   'Cause I'm most wild about my jelly roll.

   Gypsy done told me: "Don't you wear no black,"
   Yes she done told me: "Don't you wear no black,"
   Go to St. Louis, you can win him back.

   Help me to Cairo, make St. Louis by myself,
   Gone to Cairo, find my old friend Jeff.
   Goin' to pin myself close to his side,
   If I flag his train, I sure can ride.

   I love that man like a schoolboy loves his pie,
   Like a Kentucky Colonel loves his mint and rye.
   I'll love my baby till the day I die.

3. You ought to see that stovepipe brown of mine,
   Like he owns the diamond Joseph line.
   He'd make a cross-eyed old man go stone blind.

   Blacker than midnight, teeth like flags of truce,
   Blackest man in the whole St. Louis.
   Blacker the berry, sweeter is the juice.

   About a crap game, he knows a powerful lot,
   But when work time comes, he's on the dot,
   Goin' to ask him for a cold ten spot,
   What it takes to get it, he's certainly got.

   A black-headed gal make a freight train jump the track,
   Said a black-headed gal make a freight train jump the track.
   But a red-headed woman makes a preacher ball the jack.

STELLA MAE

Words and Music by
JOHN LEE HOOKER

Medium Shuffle

1.,6. Stel - la Mae, I love you,
2. Mae, you changed my drink to milk and creme.
3.-5. *(See additional lyrics)*

ba - by. I did it, I did it, Stel-la Mae, just for you, 'cause I love

I love you, — ba - by. I'd

I love you, Stel - la

do an - y-thing you asked me to, 'cause I love

Mae. *Spoken:* I'd do an - y-thing for you,

you. 'cause I love you. Stel - la

'cause I love you.

(Instrumental)

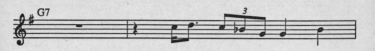

Ba - by! Oo _____

Oo ____

CODA **Repeat and Fade**

'cause I love ____ you. ____

Additional Lyrics

3. Now, Stella Mae, if you told me to jump in the ocean,
   I know I can't swim, but I'd try to do it just for you.
   Because I love you, I love you, Stella Mae.

4. Now, baby, you made me stop gambling;
   You made me stop staying up all night long.
   Now, Stella Mae, I did all these things, I did them just for you.
   'Cause I love you, I love you, oh yeah.

5. Now Stella Mae, if I had my choice for the whole round world,
   I, I, baby, I'd tell you to be my choice.
   'Cause I love you, 'cause I love you, 'cause I love you.

   (fade)

STILL GOT THE BLUES

**Words and Music by
GARY MOORE**

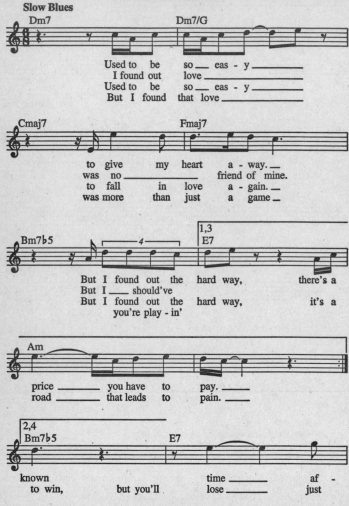

Slow Blues

Dm7 / Dm7/G

Used to be so — eas - y ——————
I found out love ——————————
Used to be so — eas - y ——————
But I found that love ——————————

Cmaj7 / Fmaj7

to give my heart a - way. —
was no —————— friend of mine.
to fall in love a - gain. —
was more than just a game. —

Bm7♭5 — 4 — / 1,3 E7

But I found out the hard way, there's a
But I —— should've
But I found out the hard way, it's a
you're play - in'

Am

price —————— you have to pay. ——
road —————— that leads to pain. ——

2,4 Bm7♭5 / E7

known time —————— af -
to win, but you'll lose —————— just

201

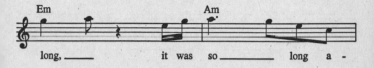

ter time. _____
the same. _____ }
So _____

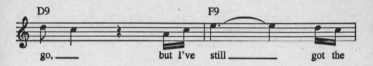

long, _____ it was so _____ long a -

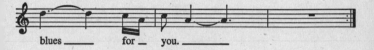

go, _____ but I've still _____ got the

blues _____ for _ you. _____

So man-y years since I've seen your

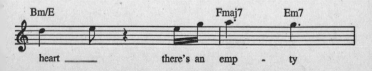

face, _____ but here in my _

heart _____ there's an emp - ty

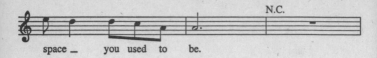

space __ you used to be.

So ___ long, ___ it was

so ___ long a - go, ___ but I've

still ___ got the blues ___ for you. ___

Though the days ___ come and

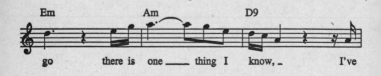

go there is one ___ thing I know, _ I've

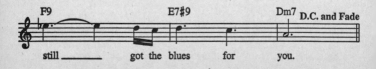

still ___ got the blues for you.

THE SKY IS CRYING

Words and Music by
ELMORE JAMES

Slow Blues tempo

1. The sky is cry-in', __ look at the tears roll down the
2.,3. *(See additional lyrics)*

street. __ The sky is cry-in', __

look at the tears roll down the street. __

I been look-ing for my ba - by, __ and I won-der where can she

be. __

2. I saw my
3. I got a

Additional Lyrics

2. I saw my baby early one morning, she was walking on down the street.
   I saw my baby early one morning, she was walking on down the street.
   You know it hurt me so bad, it made my poor heart skip a beat.

3. I got a bad feelin', my baby don't love me no more.
   I got a bad feelin', my baby don't love me no more.
   You know the sky is cryin', the tears rolling down my nose.

STORMY WEATHER
(Keeps Rainin' All the Time)

Lyric by TED KOEHLER
Music by HAROLD ARLEN

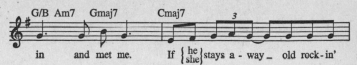

in and met me. If {he she} stays a - way _ old rock-in'

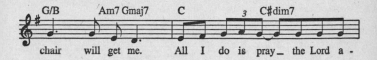

chair will get me. All I do is pray _ the Lord a -

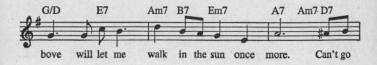

bove will let me walk in the sun once more. Can't go

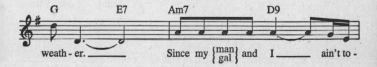

on, _____ ev-'ry-thing I had is gone, storm-y

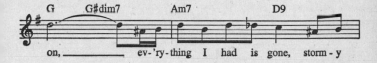

weath - er. _____ Since my {man gal} and I _____ ain't to -

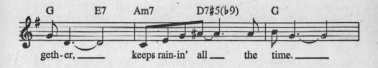

geth-er, _____ keeps rain-in' all ___ the time. _____

Keeps rain-in' all ___ the time. _____

SUGAR BLUES

Words by LUCY FLETCHER
Music by CLARENCE WILLIAMS

Gm7   C7   F   A7   Dm

lay   me   down and   die.   You   can

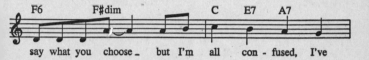

F6   F#dim   C   E7   A7

say what you   choose _   but I'm   all   con - fused, I've

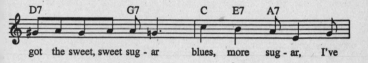

D7   G7   C   E7   A7

got   the sweet, sweet sug - ar   blues,   more   sug - ar,   I've

D7   G7   1 C Cdim G7   G7#5

got   the sweet, sweet sug - ar   blues. _____ I've got the

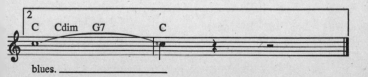

2 C Cdim   G7   C

blues. _____

SWEET SIXTEEN

Words and Music by B.B. KING and JOE BIHARI

Moderate Blues tempo

1. When I first met you, ba - by,
2.-5. *(See additional lyrics)*

ba - by, you were just ___ sweet six -

teen. When I

first met you, ba - by, ba - by, you were just ___ sweet six -

teen. ___ You just left your

G7   F7

home then, wom-an,   oh,_____ the sweet-est thing I'd

C7   1 - 4   5

ev-er seen.____   2. But you ____

Additional Lyrics

2. But you wouldn't do nothing, babe, you wouldn't do anything I ask you to.
   You wouldn't do nothing for me, baby, you wouldn't do anything
      I asked you to.
   You know you ran away from your home, baby, you want to
      run away from me.

3. You know I love you, baby, and I'll do anything you tell me to.
   You know I love you, baby, and I'll do anything you tell me to.
   There ain't nothing in the world, woman, that I wouldn't do for you.

4. I just got back from Vietnam, and I'm a long way from New Orleans.
   I just got back from Vietnam, and I'm a long way from New Orleans.
   I'm having so much trouble, baby, I wonder what in the world is gonna
      happen to me.

5. Treat me mean, baby, but I'll keep on loving you.
   You can treat me mean, baby, but I'll keep loving you just the same.
   But one of these days, baby, you're gonna give a lot of money to hear
      someone call my name.

TAIN'T NOBODY'S
BIZ-NESS IF I DO

Words and Music by PORTER GRAINGER
and EVERETT ROBBINS

TERRAPLANE BLUES

Words and Music by
ROBERT JOHNSON

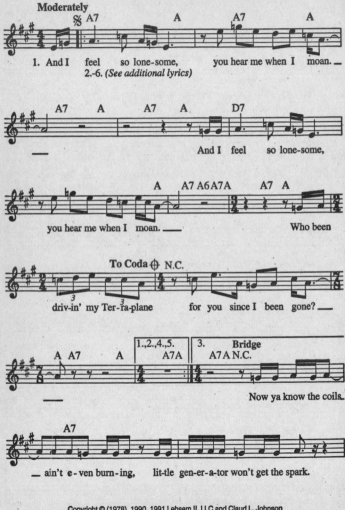

Moderately

1. And I feel so lone-some, you hear me when I moan. —

2.-6. *(See additional lyrics)*

And I feel so lone-some,

you hear me when I moan. —— Who been

driv-in' my Ter-ra-plane for you since I been gone? ——

Now ya know the coils

—— ain't e-ven burn-ing, lit-tle gen-er-a-tor won't get the spark.

All's in a bad con - di - tion, you got - ta have ___

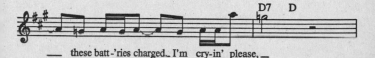

___ these batt -'ries charged. I'm cry-in' please, ___

please! _____ Don't do me wrong! _

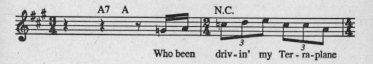

Who been driv-in' my Ter - ra-plane

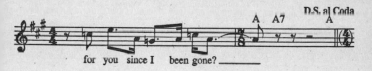

for you since I been gone? ___

and your spark plug-'ll give me fire ___

Additional Lyrics

2. I'd said I flash your lights, mama—your horn won't even blow.
   (Spoken:) 'Somebody's been runnin' my batteries down on this machine.
   I even flash my lights, mama—this horn won't even blow.
   Got a short in this connection—hoo-well, babe, it's way down below.

3. I'm 'on' h'ist your hood, mama—I'm bound to check your oil.
   I'm gon' h'ist your hood, mama-mmm—I'm bound to check your oil.
   I got a woman that I'm lovin'—way down in Arkansas.

   BRIDGE:

4. Mr. Highwayman—plea(h)ease—don't block the road.
   Puh-hee-hee-plea-(h)ease—don't block the road.
   'Cause she's re'ist'rin' a cold one hundred–
   And I'm booked and I got to go.

5. Mmm-mmm— mmm— mmm— mmm—
   You-oo-oooo-ooo— You hear me weep and moan.
   Who been drivin' my Terraplane now for–
   You-hoo– since I been gone.

6. I'm 'on' get deep down in this connection–
   Keep on tanglin' with your wires.
   I'm 'on' get deep down in this connection–
   Hoo-well, keep on tanglin' with those wires.
   And when I mash down on your little starter–
   Then your spark plug'll give me fire.

SWEET HOME CHICAGO

Words and Music by
ROBERT JOHNSON

1. Oh, — ba-by don't you want to go. —
2.–5. (See additional lyrics)

Oh, — ba-by don't you want to

go, — back to the land of Cal-i-for-nia, — to my

sweet home Chi-ca-go. —

Additional Lyrics

2. Now, one and one is two, two and two is four.
   I'm heavy loaded, baby, I'm booked, I gotta go.
   Cryin' baby, honey, don't you want to go,
   Back to the land of California, to my sweet home Chicago.

3. Now two and two is four, four and two is six.
   You gon' keep on monkeyin' 'round here,
   Friend-boy, you gon' get your business all in a trick.
   I'm cryin' baby, honey, don't you want to go,
   Back to the land of California, to my sweet home Chicago.

4. Now six and two is eight, eight and two is ten.
   Friend-boy, she trick you one time, sure she gon' do it again.
   I'm cryin' hey, hey, baby, don't you want to go,
   To the land of California, to my sweet home Chicago.

5. I'm goin' to California, from there to Des Moines, Iowa.
   Somebody will tell me that you need my help someday.
   Cryin' hey, hey, baby, don't you want to go,
   Back to the land of California, to my sweet home Chicago.

TEXAS FLOOD

Words and Music by LARRY DAVIS
and JOSEPH W. SCOTT

Moderate Blues

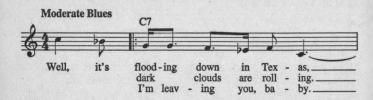

Well, it's flood-ing down in Tex - as,
dark clouds are roll - ing.
I'm leav - ing you, ba - by.

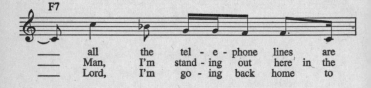

all the tel - e - phone lines are
Man, I'm stand - ing out here in the
Lord, I'm go - ing back home to

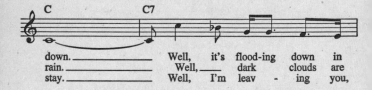

down. Well, it's flood-ing down in
rain. Well, dark clouds are
stay. Well, I'm leav - ing you,

THE THINGS THAT I USED TO DO

Words and Music by
EDDIE "GUITAR SLIM" JONES

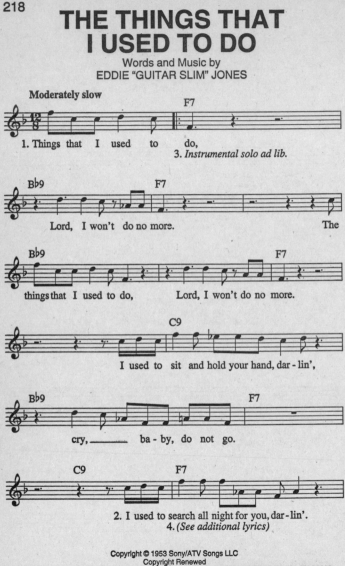

Moderately slow

F7

1. Things that I used to do,

3. *Instrumental solo ad lib.*

Bb9   F7

Lord, I won't do no more.   The

Bb9   F7

things that I used to do,   Lord, I won't do no more.

C9

I used to sit and hold your hand, dar - lin',

Bb9   F7

cry, _____ ba - by, do not go.

C9   F7

2. I used to search all night for you, dar - lin'.
4. *(See additional lyrics)*

Lord, my search would al - ways end in vain.

Lord, my search would al - ways end in vain.

I used to search all night for you, dar - lin'.

But I knew all the time, dar - lin',

that you was hid out wit' your oth - er man.

Noth - in' I can do to please you, dar - lin'.

Oh, I just can't get a - long wit' you.

Additional Lyrics

4. I'm goin' to send you back to your mama, darlin'.
Lord, I'm goin' back to my family, too.
I'm goin' to send you back to your mama, darlin'.
Lord, I'm goin back to my family, too.
Nothin' I can do to please you, darlin'.
Oh, I just can't get along wit' you.

32-20 BLUES

Words and Music by
ROBERT JOHNSON

Moderately

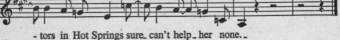

1. I sent ___ for my ba - by, and she don't
2.-7. *(See additional lyrics)*

come. I sent ___ for my ba - by,

man, and she don't come. All the doc-

- tors in Hot Springs sure ___ can't help ___ her none. ___

Additional Lyrics

2. And if she gets unruly, thinks she don't want do. *(2 times)*
   Take my 32-20, and cut her half in two.

3. She got a thirty-eight special, but I believe it's most too light. *(2 times)*
   I got a 32-20, got to make the camps alright.

4. If I send for my baby, man, and she don't come, *(2 times)*
   All the doctors in Hot Springs sure can't help her none.

5. I'm gonna shoot my pistol, gonna shoot my Gatlin' gun. *(2 times)*
   You made me love you, now your man done come.

6. Ah baby, where you stay last night? *(2 times)*
   You got your hair all tangles, and you ain't talkin' right.

7. Got a thirty-eight special, boys, it do very well. *(3 times)*

THREE HOURS PAST MIDNIGHT

Words and Music by JOHNNY WATSON
and SAUL BIHARI

Additional Lyrics

2. Yes, I tossed and tumbled on my pillow, but I just can't close eyes. *(2 times)*
   If my baby don't come back pretty quick, yes, I just can't be satisfied.

3. Well, I want my baby, I want her by my side. *(2 times)*
   Well, if she don't come home pretty soon, yes, I just can't be satisfied.

THREE O'CLOCK BLUES

Words and Music B.B. KING
and JULES BIHARI

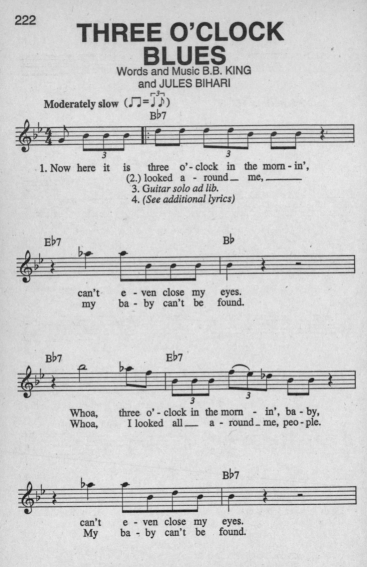

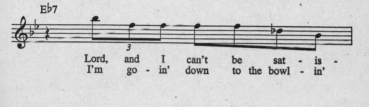

Well, I can't find my ba - by.
Well, if I don't find my ba - by,

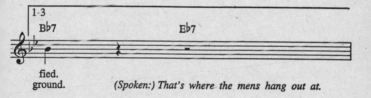

Lord, and I can't be sat - is -
I'm go - in' down to the bowl - in'

1-3

fied.
ground. *(Spoken:) That's where the mens hang out at.*

2. Lord, I've sins.

Additional Lyrics

4. Whoa, goodbye everybody, Lord, I believe this is the end.
   Whoa, goodbye everybody, Lord, I believe this is the end.
   Well, you can tell my baby to forgive me for my sins.

THE THRILL IS GONE

Words and Music by ROY HAWKINS
and RICK DARNELL

Slow Blues tempo

1. The thrill is gone, _ the thrill is gone _ a-
2.-4. *(See additional lyrics)*

way. the thrill is gone, _____ ba-by,

the thrill is gone _____ a-way. _

You know you done me wrong, _ ba-by, _ and you'll be sor-

ry some-day. _

1-3
F#7

4
F#7

Additional Lyrics

2. The thrill is gone, it's gone away from me. *(2 times)*
Although I'll still live on, but so lonely I'll be.

3. The thrill is gone, it's gone away for good. *(2 times)*
Someday I know I'll be over it all, baby, just like I know a good man should.

4. You know I'm free, free now, baby, I'm free from your spell. *(2 times)*
And now that it's all over, all I can do is wish you well.

WALKIN' BLUES

Words and Music by
ROBERT JOHNSON

1. I woke up this morn-in', — feel-in' 'round for my shoes.
2.-4. *(See additional lyrics)*

Know by that. I got these old walk-ing blues, well. Woke this morn-in'

feel 'round for my shoes.. But you know —

— by that, — I got these — old walk-ing

blues.

2. Well, blues.
3. Well
4. She got a

Additional Lyrics

2. Well, leave this mornin' if I have to ride the blinds.
   I feel mistreated, and I don't mind dyin'.
   Leave this morning, if I have to ride the blind.
   Babe, I been mistreated, and I don't mind dyin'.

3. Well, some people tell me that the worried blues ain't bad.
   Worst old feelin' I most ever had.
   People tell me that these old worried blues ain't bad.
   It's the worst old feelin', I most ever had.

4. She got a elgin movement from her head down to her toes.
   Break in on a dollar most anywhere she goes.
   Ooh, to her head down to her toes.
   Lord, she break in on a dollar, most anywhere she goes.

TROUBLE IN MIND

Words and Music by
RICHARD M. JONES

WALKING BY MYSELF

By JAMES A. LANE

Moderately fast

Walk - in' _____ by ___ my - self, ___ I

hope you un - der - stand. ___ I ___ just want to

be your lov - ing man. _____ I

love you, ___ yes, ___ I love you. It's

been my heart and soul. _____

Won't mis - treat you for your weight in gold. __

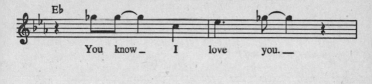

You know — I love you. —

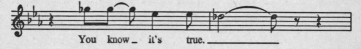

You know — it's true. _____

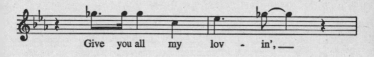

Give you all my lov - in', —

what more _____ can I do? —

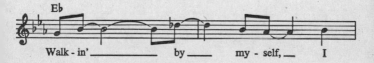

Walk - in' _____ by — my - self, — I

hope you un - der - stand. — I — just want to

be your lov - ing man. _____

WANG DANG DOODLE

Written by WILLIE DIXON

Moderate Blues feel

Tell Au - to - mat - ic Slim, ___ tell

Ra - zor Tot - in' Jim. ___ Tell

Butch - er Knife Tot - in' An - nie, tell

Fast Talk - in' Fan - nie.

We gon - na pitch a ball, ___ a down

to that un - ion hall. ___ We gon - na

romp and tromp till mid - night, we gon - na

fuss and fight — till day - light. We gon - na

pitch a —— wang dang doo - dle all night

Chorus

long. All night

long, all night long.

All night long, all night

long. We gon - na pitch a —— wang dang

doo-dle all night long. Tell

233

kick down all the doors. We gon - na

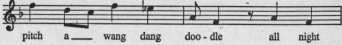

pitch a wang dang doo - dle all night

Chorus

long. All night

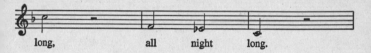

long, all night long.

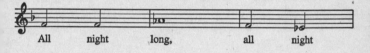

All night long, all night

long. We gon - na pitch a wang dang

D.S. and Fade on Chorus

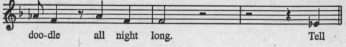

doo-dle all night long. Tell

Additional Lyrics

Tell Fats and Washboard Sam that everybody gon' jam.
Tell Shakin' Boxcar Joe, we got sawdust on the flo'.
Tell Peg and Caroline Din', we gonna have a heck of a time.
And when the fish scent fills the air, there'll be snuff juice everywhere.
Chorus

WHO DO YOU LOVE

Words and Music by
ELLAS McDANIEL

I walk for-ty-sev-en miles of barb wire, use a co-bra snake for a neck-tie, got a brand-new house on the road-side made from rat-tle-snake hide. I got a brand-new chim-ney made on top, made from a hu-man skull. Now come on, ba-by, let's take a lit-tle walk and tell me,

You should have heard just what I seen. Now

3 times

who do you love? ___

Who do you love? ___ I got a

tomb - stone hand, a grave - yard mine, I

lived long e - nough and I ain't scared o' dy - in'.

3 times

Who do you love? ___

Who do you love? ___

WHEN YOU GOT
A GOOD FRIEND

Words and Music by
ROBERT JOHNSON

1. When you got a good friend, that will stay right by your side.
2.–5. *(See additional lyrics)*

When you got a good friend,

that will stay right by your side.

Give her all of your spare time,

love and treat her right.

Additional Lyrics

2. I mistreat my baby, and I can't see no reason why. *(2 times)*
Every time I think about it, I just wring my hands and cry.

3. Wonder, could I bear apologize, or would she sympathize with me.
Mmm, would she sympathize with me.
She's a brownskin woman, just as sweet as a girlfriend can be.

4. Mmm, babe, I may be right or wrong.
Baby, it your opinion, I may be right or wrong.
Watch your close friend, baby, you enemies can't do you no harm.

5. When you got a good friend that will stay right by your side. *(2 times)*
Give her all of your spare time, love and treat her right.

WHY I SING THE BLUES

Words and Music by
B.B. KING

Moderately

Ev - 'ry - bod - y wants to know why I sing the blues.

Yes, I say

ev - 'ry - bod - y wants to know

why I sing the blues.

Well, I've been a - round a long time,

I real - ly have paid my dues.

1. When I

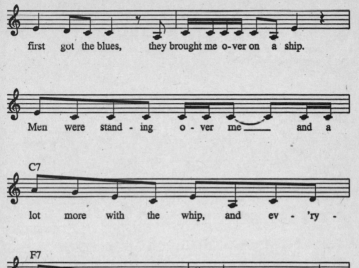

first got the blues, they brought me o-ver on a ship.

Men were stand - ing o - ver me ___ and a

C7

lot more with the whip, and ev - 'ry -

F7

bod-y wan-na know why I sing the

C

blues. Well, I've been a -

G7 **F7**

round a long ___ time, umm ___ I real - ly paid my

C **Csus**

dues. ___ 2. I've

laid   in   the ghetto flats;   cold _____ and numb.   I

4., 5. *(See additional lyrics)*

heard   the   rats   tell_ bed - bugs _____ to

give   the   roach - es   some,   and   ev - 'ry -

bod-y wan-na know   why   I   sing   the

blues.   Well, I've been a -

round a   long_ time,   umm_   I   real - ly paid my

dues. _____   3. I

stood in ___ line down in the coun-ty hall. I

heard a man say we are go - ing to

build some new a - part - ments for y'all and

ev 'ry-body wan-na know why I sing the

blues. Well, I've been a -

round a long ___ time, umm ___ I real - ly paid my

dues. ___ My

Additional Lyrics

4. My kid's gonna grow up, gonna grow up to be a fool,
   'Cause they ain't got no more room, no more room for him in school,
   And everybody wants to know, why I sing the blues.
   I say I've been around a long time, yes, I've really paid my dues.

5. Yea, you know the company told me, yes, you're born to lose,
   Everybody around feel it, seems like everybody's got the blues,
   But I had them a long time. I really, really paid my dues.
   You know I ain't ashamed of it, people, I just love to sing the blues.

YOU NEED LOVE

Written by WILLIE DIXON

You are fret - tin' and I am pet - tin'; lot of good play - in', oh, ___ you ain't get - tin'. ___ Ba - by, way down in - side. ___ Wom-an, you need love, wom-an, you need love, you've got to have some love, I'm gon-na give you some love, I know you need love.

YOU SHOOK ME

Written by WILLIE DIXON
and J.B. LENOIR

just like a hur - ri-cane.

You know you moved me, _ ba - by,

just like a hur - ri-cane. Oh,____

you know_ you move _ me sweet-heart, just like an earth-quake. do the

land. Oh, _____

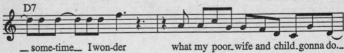

_ some-time_ I won-der what my poor_ wife and child_ gonna do._

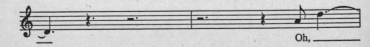

Oh, _____

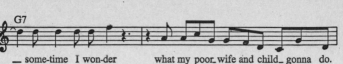

_ some-time I won-der   what my poor wife and child_ gonna do.

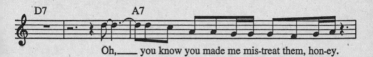

Oh,____ you know you made me mis-treat them, hon-ey.

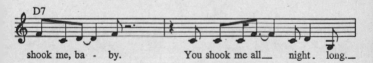

Oh, _____ I'm mad - ly in love with you.

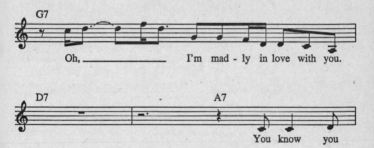

You know   you

shook me, ba - by.   You shook me all__ night . long.__

__   Mm. _____

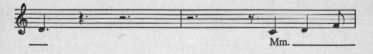

__   You shook me all __ night long.

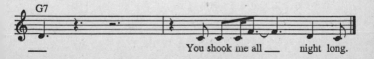

GUITAR CHORD FRAMES

	C	Cm	C+	C6	Cm6
C					

	C#	C#m	C#+	C#6	C#m6
C#/D♭		4fr		3fr	2fr

	D	Dm	D+	D6	Dm6
D					

	E♭	E♭m	E♭+	E♭6	E♭m6
E♭/D#	3fr		× ○○×		

	E	Em	E+	E6	Em6
E					

	F	Fm	F+	F6	Fm6
F					

This guitar chord reference includes 120 commonly used chords. For a more complete guide to guitar chords, see "THE PAPERBACK CHORD BOOK" (HL00702009).

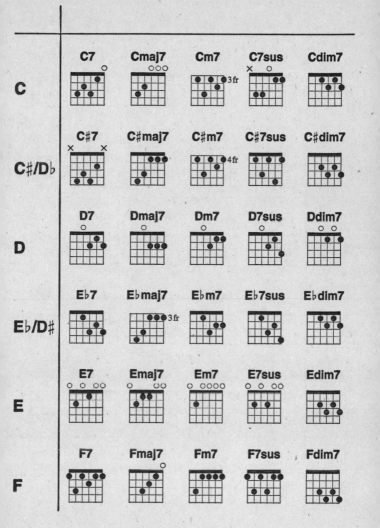

250

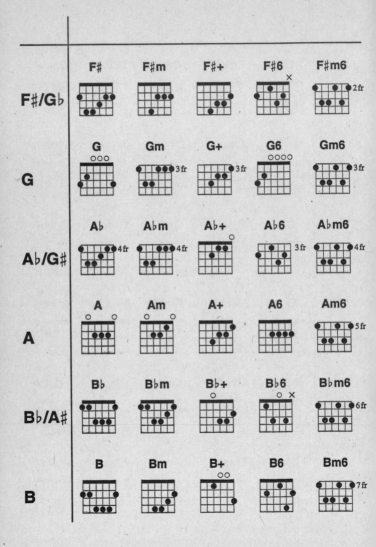

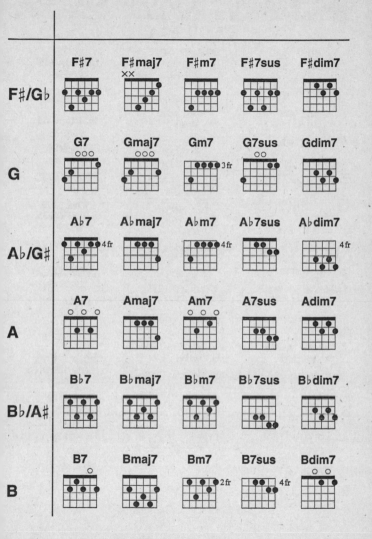

THE PAPERBACK SONGS SERIES

$7.95 EACH

THE '20s
00240236

THE '30s
00240238

THE '40s
00240239

THE '50s
00240240

THE '60s
00240241

THE '70s
00240242

THE '80s
00240243

THE '90s
00240244

'80s & '90s ROCK
00240126

THE BEACH BOYS
00240261

THE BEATLES
00702008

BIG BAND SWING
00240171

THE BLUES
00702014

BROADWAY SONGS
00240157

CHILDREN'S SONGS
00240149

CHORDS FOR KEYBOARD & GUITAR
00702009

CHRISTMAS CAROLS
00240142

CHRISTMAS SONGS
00240208

CLASSIC ROCK
00310058

CLASSICAL THEMES
00240160

CONTEMPORARY CHRISTIAN
00240245

COUNTRY HITS
00702013

NEIL DIAMOND
00702012

GOOD OL' SONGS
00240159

GOSPEL SONGS
00240143 ($8.95)

HYMNS
00240103

INTERNATIONAL FOLKSONGS
00240104

JAZZ STANDARDS
00240114 ($8.95)

BILLY JOEL
00240267

ELTON JOHN
00240257

LATIN SONGS
00240156

LOVE SONGS
00240150

MORE JAZZ STANDARDS
00240269

MOTOWN HITS
00240125

MOVIE MUSIC
00240113

POP/ROCK
00240179

ELVIS PRESLEY
00240102

ROCK & ROLL COLLECTION
00702020

RODGERS & HAMMERSTEIN
00240177

SOUL HITS
00240178

TV THEMES
00240170

FOR MORE INFORMATION, SEE YOUR LOCAL MUSIC DEALER,
OR WRITE TO:

HAL•LEONARD®
CORPORATION
7777 W. BLUEMOUND RD. P.O. BOX 13819 MILWAUKEE, WI 53213

www.halleonard.com

0206

Prices, availability and contents subject to change without notice. Some products may not be available outside the U.S.A.